HOLY WAR AGAINST THE HOLY

David Serafim

HOLY WAR AGAINST THE HOLY

Copyright © David Serafim 2023

This book is a work of non-fiction

Title: Holy War Against the Holy
Author: David Serafim
Cover: David Serafim
Iconography:
Wikimedia Commons (Public Domain)
The Noun Project (Royalty Free License)
Worldmap from Wikimedia Commons by Dark Tea (Creative Commons License)
Map of Europe from freeworldmaps (https://freeworldmaps.net/printable/europe/)
Iceberg Image by Simon Lee (Unsplash License)
All other graphics by David Serafim
ISBN: 978-0-9756344-7-9

In Memoriam
Maria Helena Varela Santos (1934-2020)

"But seek ye first the Kingdom of God and His righteousness, and all these things shall be added unto you. "

Contents

HOLY WAR AGAINST THE HOLY

CHAPTER 1

The Atheist Delusion

THE EQUIVOCATION FALLACY

a binary answer

It's been made evident that the starting point for modern atheism (or *new* atheism as it's often referred to) is founded on fuzzy logic, being utilized as a means to escape the objective problems that are attached to this belief system. But to establish atheism as such, one must first begin with the origins of the word *theism*. It is derived from the Ancient Greek *theos*, meaning God (or gods), with the word itself referring to the cause or source of everything there is: all material and all immaterial things. Theism is thereby the active stance of believing there is a God, no matter how it is defined, or even if the belief is carried without any particular definition. One could hold the belief there is something beyond the physical realm we inhabit, yet choose not to define it. However, most people do. Antithetically, atheism pertains to an active stance of denial. The belief is still there, but it is a negative one this time round. The latter therefore exists as a direct counterpoint to the idea of a supreme being or entity that delivered or created the universe, whether through a state of immanence or self-existence.

Gnosticism is defined as the act of embracing spiritual knowledge, i.e. knowledge that does not originate from the scientific process. Therefore it's counterpart, *agnosticism,* is the rejection of such embrace, leaving the adherent with means to questioning the ethereal but without necessarily doing so, forcing him into a neutral stance. Both the theist and the atheist hold spiritual knowledge, by providing an answer to matters transcendental to science. They both use faith to reach a conclusion that allows for a final determination in respect to this subject. It's more appealing to any individual to avoid indifference because it allows him to come to terms with one of the biggest questions dwelling in the human mind – if not the greatest.

To summarize, when asked the question "Do you believe in God?" or "Is there a God?", the agnostic abstains from providing an answer that carries certainty. He can simply say "I do not know"; whereas the gnostic needs to give an answer that confers resolution to the matter: "Yes", says the one who believes, and "No", says the one who believes not. But the answer is binary, as opposed to having an aggregate of options and paths, as many atheists misleadingly, conveniently and exhaustively suggest. They need a smoke-and-mirrors strategy to try avoid exposure when being made to address the debilities of their own faith, or the fact it is a faith in the slightest.

Agnosticism is a stance that requires neutrality regarding metaphysical affairs, leading to the devotion and focus on physical ones. Atheism leads to the same behavior regarding devotion to physical affairs, but it is based to an act of negative faith that declares God not to exist. Theism opens the door to worship through the act of positive faith. **Figure 1** compacts these three different positions into a chart that makes things crystal clear. Only acceptance of this fact brings closure to such a simple concern, yet so indelibly important to our species, as opposed to diving into the disarray of blending the word *agnostic* with *atheist* and *theist,* rendering them moot and purposeless, or at very least disorienting. Both atheism and theism infer faith and cannot therefore be simultaneously used alongside agnosticism.

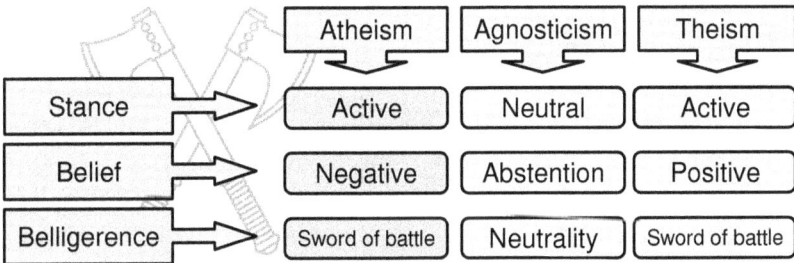

	Atheism	Agnosticism	Theism
Stance	Active	Neutral	Active
Belief	Negative	Abstention	Positive
Belligerence	Sword of battle	Neutrality	Sword of battle

Figure 1: Spiritual belief without the clutter

It must be added, the agnostic focus solely on scientific affairs due to refraining from attempting to acquire spiritual knowledge, as it abstains from meddling in transcendental concerns, but always leaving the door in the open to whether they exist or not. In contrast, the atheist has made a decision involving that very knowledge and, having found a resolution about it through an act of faith, turns to science as the only avenue to acquire knowledge. As such their divergence comes from the narrow mindedness atheism enforces versus the open mindedness agnosticism demands.

THE PRECEDENCY OF FAITH

the privilege of belief

A question then must be asked: why the need for modern atheists to clutch onto an equivocation fallacy, i.e. dismembering the significance of the word into multiple ones? The answer comes easy: because assigning multiple meanings to the word *atheism* is extremely useful in order to create confusion or diffusion, thereby using it as a stratagem for deflection. So much for them being proponents of the scientific method and the objective pursuit of truth. Calling several different things by the same name allows them to shape-shift when entering debate with theists – furthermore it supplies atheists with a sword of battle they can use to attack, scorn and deride religious affairs. This can constitute a major advantage over the agnostic, who's humility clashes with atheistic arrogance, because any signs of doubt would make the latter look undecided and weak. This fallacy allows for the atheist to hop from one stance to the other, often by declaring to just "lack gods", then shifting into a stance of persistently attacking scripture, religious dogma and doctrine. Attacking religion is a form of action, not indifference or neutrality. To put it bluntly, the equivocation fallacy is a coward's way out from the atheist's camp to avoid confrontation by introducing many shades of gray. But in the end of the day we are dealing with a question that requires a simple binary answer, or abstention from specifying one.

Faith is defined as *the belief in something without proof,* which is to say a stance taken due to the lack of scientific evidence, therefore bringing answers to questions that science has not been able to handle – and maybe never will. This confers atheists as believers and, consequently, atheism as a belief system. This is a degree of logical reasoning from which they cannot escape, no matter how hard their struggle. Science is in fact the wrong tool for the job, as it relies on empirical data to constitute fact, thus rendering it useless when it comes to the topic of the ethereal, the transcendental, the immaterial. To the atheist, faith must precede scientific knowledge, as it is the very belief that there is no exogenous element to the universe that leads him to devote himself solely to the scientific method. It would be nonsensical for the atheist to depend on the acquiring of scientific evidence to reach a conclusion about God: not only any data regarding the existence of God isn't available but if it were, wouldn't we all be forced to accept it? The atheist simply opted to take the reductivist approach and declared preemptively that all things, all answers, all knowledge must come from the realm of the material – the universe made of space and time – as he rejects the existence or any idea of God through a belief that precedes anything scientific. Waiting for fact, only to then take a stance based on whatever is scientifically established is the path of agnosticism, which rejects any preemptive act of faith due to its neutral nature.

There is also the issue of contradiction, where many modern atheists, especially the more renowned ones such as Richard Dawkins, Sam Harris or Michael Shermer, keep shape-shifting by declaring doubt, or introducing gauges that allow uncertainty, only to then confess "They don't believe in God", or "More and more people are realizing God does not exist". It's blatant their 'doubt' is not, and will never be, supported by any empirical data, but is instead simply a mask they hide under, to avoid being confronted with the reality of their creed – they are indeed people of faith.

THE ETYMOLOGICAL ARGUMENT

from dirt till dawn

The etymological definition of the word *atheism* is clean-cut but it has been diluted in games that are treasonous to logic and reason. Thrown into a circle of confusion – an atheist's favorite – the sharpness of the word was lost, and vague explanations branching into different directions took over. The prefix *A* in the Ancient Greek language, when attached to a word, indicates the antithetical meaning of the original word: it is used to represent the exact opposite significance of such word, corresponding to the rejection of what the original word was trying to signify in the first place.

     For example, if one were to refer to an achromatic image (an image perceived to have zero color saturation, therefore made of shades of gray), no-one will deduce that it *may* or *may not* have color; if one were to mention there is an abyss ahead, there would be no doubt that it would be a bottomless pit, even though due to the lack of existence of such it is usually inferred that its euphemistic in nature and would actually mean the bottom of the pit is not visible, or at least that it lies far beneath. Accordingly, atheism refers to the affirmation of the non-existence of God – *any* God. Even the word *atom* stands for *indivisible*, i.e. that which cannot be split into smaller parts. There is no misconception about this etymological argument, other than the one modern atheists conveniently introduce to manipulate the word to their benefit.

One of the founding fathers of atheism, the Greek philosopher Democritus (460 – 370 B.C.), described it with the idiom "The universe is atoms and empty space, everything else is opinion" – or for a modernized version we could say "The universe is space and time, everything else is subjective". In other words, according to atheism nothing exists outside the material world. That was the original design and intent of the word along with its etymological structure, reflecting necessity to express a perspective of the world without resorting to gods, incorporeal entities or forces hence rejecting these altogether. There is no space for spiritual doubt or skepticism – the answer is final, and it is a negative one.

THE CIRCLE OF CONFUSION

in the middle of the sandstorm

The contemporary definitions for atheism, within the equivocation fallacy, split into *weak atheism* and *strong atheism*. In the first category, also known as *implicit atheism*, you will find people who do not care for making a decision regarding their belief when it comes to God or any ethereal matters, and people that are not capable of making that decision, such as children or even animals. However this definition is identical to that of *agnosticism*, and the very reason why it was first used in the 5th century BC in Ancient Greece: to allow one to express their views without resorting to the idea of possessing spiritual knowledge. If a child is unable to understand the abstract concept of the divine or any spiritual matters, it is inferred by default it is therefore agnostic. It does not choose because it can't reach such levels of depth in terms of this specific knowledge. An animal, unlike a human child which can mature, will never be able to delve into this type of abstract thought because it does not possess pure reason. Conversely, the act of choosing to not hold a belief leads one intentionally down the same path. The empiricist philosophical theory of *Positivism*, that insists noesis to be entirely dependent on sensory experience, should be the only avenue taken by atheists, thereby rejecting any theological or ethereal pursuit of knowledge. It must be reinforced that the agnostic does not deny the existence of God, either through lack of rational proficiency or choice, but it acknowledges that doing so would in fact be contrary to its neutral stance. The agnostic chooses not to choose, deferring any non-scientific knowledge into the realm of skepticism in a pledge of loyalty towards science, while keeping an open mind. The affirmation that God isn't knowable can only be made by people with this mindset, as any active stance will be deprived of eternal doubt – quite the opposite, it will be indeed be full of certainty.

The agnostic stance is therefore in complete contrast with that of the atheist, who embraces the act of believing there isn't a God. They relate in no way to each other, demonstrating *implicit atheism* is nothing more than a means for atheists to keep their sword of battle while pretending to be neutral – also commonly known as cheating. This form of atheism doesn't exist. It is nothing more than pure fabrication in order to get away with fuzzy logic and trickery within the circle of confusion they created and attempt to lure the ones that debate them into.

Moving onto *explicit atheism*, there are two avenues, supposedly, that can be taken: that of categorically affirming that God does not exist is scientific fact, or that of rejecting

God but accepting there is no evidence to support it. This mess can be unobstructed by dividing atheists into two groups: the ones that accept that there is no evidence to support their averment about the non-existence of God, and the ones that claim that there is such evidence. Realistically, both sides are wrong as science as nothing to do with proving the existence of the Almighty Creator of all things. We can read into these two definition simply different levels of honesty regarding their stance. The ones that claim they have enough evidence to 'prove' their claim are further away from embracing their act of faith then the ones who accept their scientific grounds are lacking.

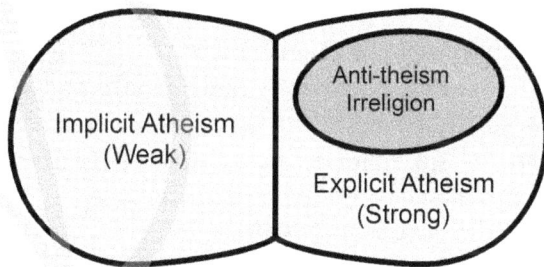

Figure 2: The atheism circle of confusion

The concept of *anti-theism* has also to be addressed, as atheists will never stop muddling things up in the name of science and reason. The idea that any atheist would not be also an anti-theist is dead absurd. If theism leads one down the trodden path of worshiping an invisible, non-existent deity, how can any atheist accept such practice? As a parallel, one could imagine granddad believes indeed there are pots of gold at the end of each rainbow, leading him to proceed to travel trying to find his imaginary reward. But shouldn't one reproach and condemn him, even out of love and care for the old man? It could be suggested at least he is getting some exercise, plus his quest makes him not only healthy but also joyful. However, couldn't one try to convince him to reach such goals through other means, which would also involve something mentally healthy? If one *believes*, or *knows*, such quest to be frivolous, and even potentially harmful due to the inevitable disappointment upon one's elderly relative becoming acquainted with reality, shouldn't it be mandatory to detract the old man from pursuing such wasteful endeavor? If one is an atheist, it stands to reason one *must* also be an anti-theist.

On the topic of being *irreligious*, one can be terse and accept that theists can also be so, even though, just like with anti-theism, atheists should always stand against the practice of religion and for the very same reasons presented above. An irreligious person is simply rejecting organized religion, but it could still maintain their connection to spirituality regardless.

Once the cloud of dust settles and is fully cleared, with all the clutter removed surrounding it, the word *atheism* along with its genuine meaning, in both its contemporary form or ancient, is easily recognizable as what was originally intended to signify: to reject from dwelling in the metaphysical by denying that any such experiences are possible. If we are fully material entities, creatures of nature and nothing else, it stands to reason to procure all answers within this physical realm instead of imaginary ones. And whereas the agnostic searches for answers only within science, keeping his mind open to the possibility or eventuality of embracing any spiritual cognition, the atheist *knows*, through his own faith, such experiences are impossible as there is nothing transcendental to science that humans can cognize. The atheist worships the void, while the agnostic leaves a big question mark regarding it.

THE TREE OF FAITH

no good tree bears bad fruit

It is possible to structure all belief systems, or lack thereof, in a vivid manner that leaves no space for doubt or cheating.

Accepting that atheism is not split into multiple definitions such as *weak* or *strong*, and that it has to necessarily be 'anti' the thing it rejects (by nature of the word), it can be concluded it is simply a *negative* belief in God – in contrast with theism which is a *positive* belief in God. This leads one into the path of lucidity by observing both belief systems branch off its root, which is gnosticism, since they both require spiritual knowledge in order to reach a conclusion. Taking this approach helps closing the matter and leave no space for doubt.

Both the belief in God and the denial of His existence can then sprawl into multiple branches: theism on one hand can lead to multiple interpretations of what or who God is; atheism on the other reaches a dead end because there is nothing to interpret. Both can nevertheless lead to organized religious movements, so called denominations, cults and orders, or in the broader sense, the 'church' – the man-made structure that is integrated into the social environment, and allows its affiliates

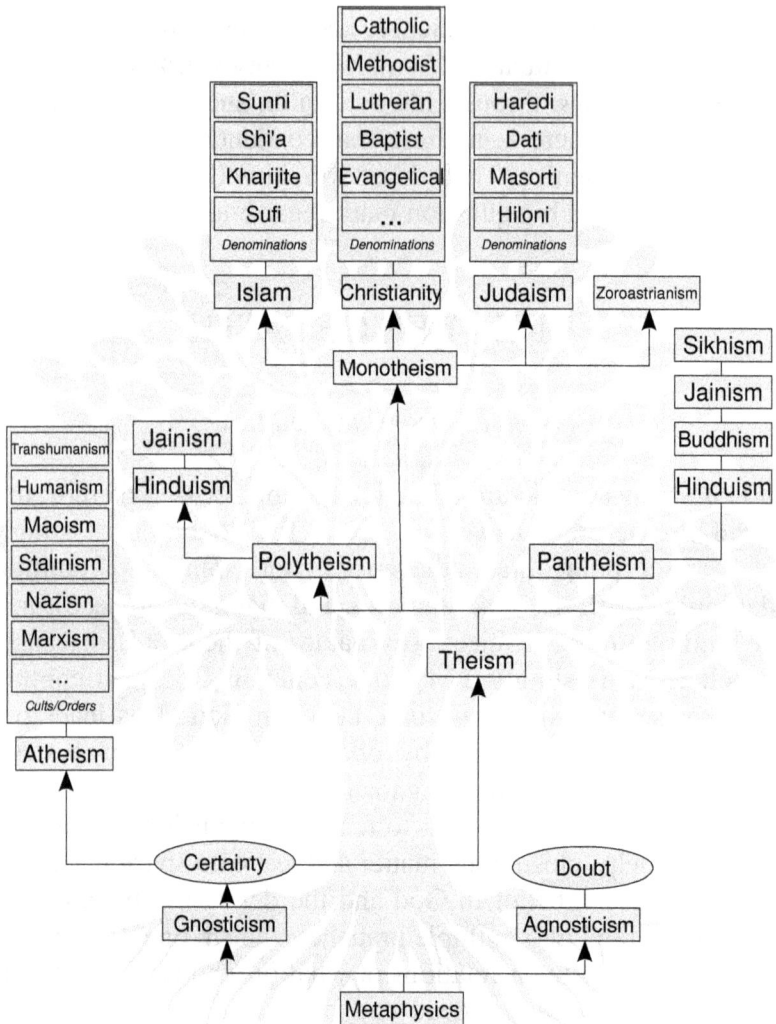

Figure 3: The Tree of Faith

to commune. Humans have the natural propensity to seek hierarchical bodies they can plunge themselves into in order to co-participate and cooperate. In the case of religion there is the need to find guidance when it comes to social norms, behavioral patterns, group acceptance and other regulatory elements. A differentiation must therefore be made between the original and objective meaning of religion and its succedaneum. In **Figure 3** a multitude of mainstream religions can be found such as Christianity, Hinduism, Islam, etc. that follow the originally designed conception of the word as *interpretations* of the metaphysical. These attempt to fill in the blanks left by the inability of science to probe into matters that it finds to be transcendental. They are then split into a variation of denominations that cater for their followers, each with their own *translation*, i.e. a specific reading or understanding of the religion they branched off.

To sum it all up, *theism* embraces the belief in God, *religion* provides an interpretation for each belief, and finally a *denomination* supplies an institutionalized structure that is directly planted into a social environment so it can furnish it with rules and principles – organized religion in a nutshell. Contrary to popular belief, this organized religion form can also apply to atheism, as it can branch off into 'churches' that appear to be unrelated to its theistic cousins but are very much the same. Humans are naturally prone to worship and, regardless of believing in a transcendental deity or not, will always seek someone or something to bow to. If the belief they hold is negative, then the worship cannot be attached to an immaterial deity, instead redirecting their veneration to another human, organization or movement. It is thus of the utmost importance to understand the true significance of the word *religion* in the spiritual sense, versus organized regulatory structures that are man-made, which can operate without any links to other-worldliness whatsoever.

DENIALISM

chameleons don't run, they hide

The persistent state of denial modern atheism leads its followers into – the main starting point that eventually leads to their irrational behavior, especially when claiming to be proponents of the scientific method – can be referred to as *denialism*. Their speech is full of grandiloquence, partiality and hubris, as if they belong to a higher cast that has seen through the obvious flaws of the fairy-tale gods imagined by religious people. In reality atheists *are* believers, they just hold a *negative* belief instead of a positive one.

The evidence is in their bias, always pending clearly towards God not existing, therefore revealing it to lack neutrally altogether. Attacking religion is a form of action, not indifference, and, as stated previously, this confers to atheists an active stance relating this issue, preventing them from engaging in any shape-shifting, i.e. changing their stance whenever it's convenient to them. If an atheist is asked whether they believe in God or not, they can always defer to the gimmicky reply "I just lack a belief in any gods", while displaying an attitude of contempt, derision and scorn towards praying, worship and any form of religious practices. This is in fact the best way to differentiate an atheist from an agnostic: the former possesses a narrow mindedness whereas the latter an open one.

As an example, if an atheist enters a bookshop and sees

two new books in the shelf, one with the name "A Universe from Nothing" another with the name "A Universe from God", which one is it reasonable to think he would most likely ignore and which one he would rush to take off the shelf to fulfill his belief? An agnostic cannot pend towards either, thence the neutral position. The question of God existing or not requires a binary answer, or an abstention. If one *believes,* the choice is made whether it is negative or positive there are no gray areas or room for doubt. Atheists cannot perceive God as a non-issue, other than that of their own resolve through belief – God isn't, so it becomes irrelevant to them.

Humans are curious by nature and they require answers to be fulfilled, including the ones about phenomena that occurs across the cosmos, in some instances without any direct influence in ours lives or civilization whatsoever. Atheists endeavor to explain everything that is experienced without resorting to God or any metaphysical arguments. They assume His non-existence, so why claim neutrality, or play cat-and-mouse games? Why the permanent state of denial – the denialism? Only to confer to them the insincere sense of authority of reason over the emotion of preference. If they pretend not to hold a belief in such matters they cannot be viewed as people of faith, and instead they can falsely present themselves as people of science.

Atheism is simply the negative belief in God. It can be read as the belief that any truth comes from material cognitive experiences our body is subjected to. It's a war waged between our sensory perceptions and the the universe's cause-and-effect, with our minds as the interpreter of what we commonly refer to as *reality.* No information we obtain can therefore originate from anything immaterial. If one were to ask if the sun will rise tomorrow, the answer would require no belief but instead, by resorting to scientific knowledge, an assertion can be made: yes, it will. No need to *believe* the sun will rise or not. In direct contrast, the question of whether God exists or not has no scientific data – and even if there were any, what good would it do? It could easily dismissed as a potential illusion created by superior lifeforms that inhabit this realm. Besides, the Creator of the universe doesn't *have* to manifest Himself in such way that convinces you of anything, no matter what the atheist's demands are. Does a cockroach demand a human to bring back a breadcrumb as the latter mops the kitchen floor? Find that the difference between us and God far surpasses that of insects and humans.

THE ATHEISM LITERAL

all or nothing

An argument that is often incorrectly presented by new atheists is that of certain religions allowing for one of their followers to be atheistic. If, say, an Hindu chooses not to believe in deities, which Hinduism allows for, then he is therefore an atheist. This is utterly ludicrous as there is a conflation of the rejection of particular gods with having no positive belief at all. Richard Dawkins claims that a Christian is an Islam atheist, and vice-versa – he couldn't have been more anti-pedagogic. This is the typical strategy of the modern atheists, as by distorting their own creed in order to suit their needs, even if in a transitory fashion, it leads to the appearance of victory in debate or lecture. The straightforward, logical, unadulterated answer is a Christian *cannot* be an atheist, because the latter is the opposition to any forms of theism, thence denying it.

Christianity, Hinduism, Islam, Sikhism, Buddhism, Judaism, etc. are all *subsets* of theism, without exception. In fact as a positive believer, a theist can actually choose not to affiliate himself with any specific religion and choose to be solely spiritual. Any perspective a theist has, any interpretation of God and the spiritual realm immediately prevents him to enter in contradiction with the atheistic point of view – the antagonistic, antithetical point of view that declares there is nothing outside the physical domain.

If looking into the universe of vehicles, for example, one could say owning a boat still would make him a vehicle owner. The same can be said for those who own a car, a motorcycle or a bicycle. All these individuals with be in possession of a vehicle, regardless of its type, even if each denies being in ownership of any other type of vehicle. Since the boat is a subcategory of vehicle, one can infer its owner can adhere to a vehicular club of sorts, making him ineligible to be classified as a non-owner – one lacking a vehicle. The same logic applies to theism, where any positive believer, regardless of his particular view on God, cannot be placed in the opposite branch of the tree, even if one's interpretation of God does not involve divine entities. Pantheism is a good example of such perception of God where there are no single supernatural beings or deities its followers resort to, but this without precluding theism, where in fact it branches from.

Atheism denies any interpretation of God, through the negation of the existence of any such ethereal concepts, rendering it impossible for a Buddhist, Hindu, etc. to belong to this family. In Ancient Greece, where the word was formulated, the thought of being religious, of being theistic, more often than not implied the worship of multiple supernatural beings with super powers that interfered with people lives, both in a positive and negative way, hence the erroneously conflation of deity with God, when in reality theism is much more all-encompassing than that narrow rendition.

The choice is mutually exclusive by nature of the question posed requiring a binary answer: do you believe or believe not? Is there a God? Is there a metaphysical source for the universe we inhabit? There are no more than two terms, two answers, two options. Agnosticism is thence suitable for the science purist, since it defers the need for an answer and instead resorts to abstention in the name of focusing on scientific inquiry. The agnostic also inherits the benefit of avoiding any tainting that could potentially, and regularly does, occur when studying the physical world, the space-time universe, due to holding the atheistic negative belief. He freed himself from the burden of faith or making a choice at all – if anything that transcends the material world does exist, it's not his business to research, nor his problem to solve.

The main reason why atheists don't defend the atheist literal meaning is due to the convenience in delving into their circle of confusion during debate or conversation. It's very useful, and disingenuous to say the least, for the atheist to monkey branch between a negative stance and a neutral one, thereby avoiding exposure. Furthermore, they refrain from addressing the idea of theism without religion, because they conflate both. A person can choose to be spiritual without enlisting in any form of religion, creed, or guild. But to the atheist it's highly favorable to present the idea of a positive belief in God as inextricably connected to religion, all under the false pretense of the pursuit of knowledge and truth.

CHAPTER 2

Hateism

A NEW TYPE OF ATHEISM

out with the good, in with the bad

The process of stepping away from holding religious views isn't natural or comforting to humans. The truth of the matter is, when Europeans colonized three-quarters of the globe they didn't find a single culture or race without any gods or spiritual leaders. Therefore to persuade people to leave such beliefs requires a lot of work, a lot of persistence and a lot of propaganda. For the atheist to proselytize, cherry-picking supposed successes of their faith isn't enough and there is also the need to put down, devalue and deride any opposing views. This process of neatly grouping the positives and separating them from the negatives is commonly labeled *motivated reasoning*, where anything inconvenient for a particular argument is selectively filtered out and binned. A campaign of hatred, mockery, deceit and propaganda is the best formula to push people away from holding any beliefs other than that of "There is no God".

The Ancient Greek philosopher Thucydides (460 – 400

B.C.) is often seen as the father of the discipline of History, that is the recording in writing and documenting human stories, events, wars, cataclysms, and so on and so forth. Always assuming it's being done with impartiality and using a strict method based on scientific evidence. To follow through this premise, when writing about the Plague of Athens (430 B.C.), he did so without resorting to any claims of divine punishment, intervention or justice, even if he himself fell victim to the epidemic. However, when writing his multi-volume *History of the Peloponnesian War,* a lot of bias is suspected to have been had in favor of Athens, a side Thucydides himself served for in the military as a general during said war against Sparta. His opinion interfered with his judgment simply because that is part of the human condition, not because he was a bad historian. Even if one is to try to show no preconception or partisanship towards a subject that is dear to him, invariably one will be victim of the pitfalls of preference and prejudice. It is nearly impossible to escape this paradigm, thence being preferable to, in an act of full humility, acknowledge one's frailty and fallibility to avoid becoming a rampant hypocrite.

A neologism can, and should due to necessity, be introduced to refer to the act of, through the aforementioned process of selectively filtering, distorting and rearranging the reality of the atheist doctrine in order to suit the needs of those of frail mind who find themselves adherents of this belief system: *faux-atheism.* The use of fuzzy logic is paramount to their success, otherwise their audience would see through all the excuses and evasive maneuvers and choose not to convert. If the convenience atheism provides over agnosticism in this holy war – a sword of battle to destroy theists – it may also lead to awful consequences due to the removal of anything spiritual from human existence. As stated, humans are naturally spiritual, and as a consequence religious, which renders societies without God problematic. Humans are reduced to being molecular structures, even sometimes the suggestion of being fully under the whims of their *selfish genes*, wholly and utterly depleting us of significance and value.

Even though modern atheists defend such ideas, and many others that lead to utilitarianism and the sort, they clearly don't seem very keen on following them. They do not practice what they preach – at least the large majority of them don't. Let's take the example of *freewill*: under the guise of atheism, because there is no soul or any metaphysical human component of any variety, atheists should by default embrace the philosophical view of *determinism,* which states that everything that occurs in the *present* is the result of a previous state (the most recent *past)* of the universe under natural law, i.e. the laws of physics that govern the universe. This assertion would lead one to see himself as nothing more than a marionette, completely submitted to the same laws that control all other atomic structures that aren't living organisms. But for the faux-atheist such is not the case as, in a convoluted manner, they try to justify their case for keeping their *libertarian freewill (*also know as *metaphysical libertarianism)* without resorting to metaphysics. This game faux-atheists play has been labeled *compatibilism.*

One doesn't have to dive too deeply into the nonsense of compatiblism to quickly realize the concocted scheme, even though it will be necessary to remove all the clutter dropped into the issue by faux-atheists – this has been done so on purpose in an attempt to add confusion to the matter to make it harder to spot the mechanics of the deception involved. The shuffle of some ideas between determinism and metaphysical libertarianism, followed by the mixing of them together as to pretend a solution has been found results in an answer that supplies them with the lie that humans, as the molecular structures they are, are now 'free'. The laws of physics themselves weren't changed, but a instead loopy line was drawn, where a simple, straight, direct line should have been. This benefits their 'theories' with plenty of muddiness and disorder, making it hard to track down the problem. "It's all too complicated" they declare as a subterfuge, when it's obvious the direct-line from A to B (as seen on **Figure 4**) would have sufficed.

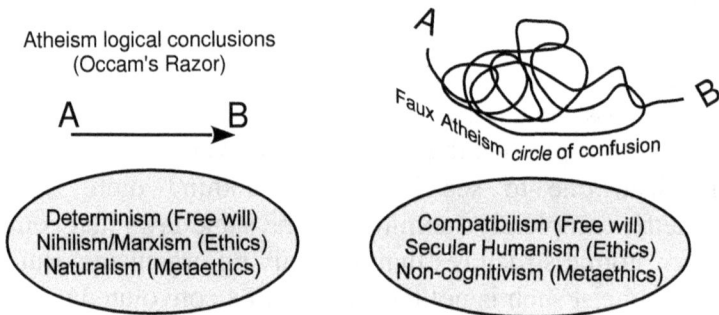

Atheism logical conclusions
(Occam's Razor)

A_____B

Determinism (Free will)
Nihilism/Marxism (Ethics)
Naturalism (Metaethics)

A

Faux Atheism circle of confusion

B

Compatibilism (Free will)
Secular Humanism (Ethics)
Non-cognitivism (Metaethics)

Figure 4: Atheist's fuzzy logic

This smoke and mirrors tactical maneuver allows the faux-atheist to purport to be a person of science while hiding belief has in fact taken over, welcoming the nonsensical approach generating confusion. Motivated reasoning is used to throw religious values and views under the bus, with the false pretense this values were always there, and the religion that gave birth to them is unnecessary and superfluous. Whatever implications of losing connection to the immaterial world can be voided outright. Moral good doesn't need spiritual laws, neither the idea of an individual's value within society, much less the concept of agency, freedom of will and existential dread – with a few sprinkles of atheistic dogma and circular logic and everything's acquires the appearance of solving all these existential conundrums.

INSTITUTIONAL RELIGION

one misconception isn't enough

Some words in human vocabulary can be ambiguous, even without malice. The word *religion* is certainly one of them, branching into two meanings when only of them can be formally recognized. Religion formally, and originally, applies to a set of principles, values and practices based on a system of doctrine built by individuals, with a view to find devotion, worship and obedience to a supernatural power: a divine entity, several deities or a force. But the other use for the word can be that of referring to a man made institution created as an hierarchical structure within society and populated by clergy in order to guide the followers of said divine power.

A congregational social organization or system can be designed under different circumstances, even when a supernatural entity or force isn't present, with the same aim of governing the masses through indoctrination. This can be referred to as the *church*, or *organized religion* for clarity. Faux-atheists use this ambiguity, without any investment to clear things out, with the ill intent of dissociating themselves of the possibility of their negative belief system being compatible with such religious organizations. Indeed atheism supports the use of such social structures, therefore asserting atheists *can* be religious in this particular sense. The defunct Stalinism, Maoism and the contemporary cult of Kim Jong-un in North Korea, are clean-cut examples of these religious expressions. For the ones who declare God not to exist but want to find some solace in post-detachment from their spirituality. Communism is a byproduct of atheism and yet most of its manifestations are structured around a *church* form, no matter how much atheists, of the *faux* kind or any other, find it disagreeable coming to terms with this realness.

Confirmation bias is abundantly used by the bishops of faux-atheism, especially when embarking in their *hateistic* campaigns, i.e. when persecuting and attacking theists through lies, diatribes and scorn, with the final intention of intermingling this concepts of organized religion into the true, and original, meaning of the *religion*: as long as they can label it as such, it is instantly dumped into the "it's religious, not atheistic" basket. If they can remove all the merits and credits from any sort of religion – of the true kind – and hijack it for themselves and, conversely, mark every of their failures as religious – of the organized kind – they can present a false narrative where they are holy and religion is the devil. Humans have the natural propensity, if not necessity, to engage in some form of worship or another, therefore justifying the incessant search for stratified authority within their society under which they can feel integrated and safe. Organized religion, also commonly referred to as the church, is as much part of the atheistic belief system as the theistic one.

Religion, in it's pure form, is not the same as spirituality or theism, but it sure depends on them. Without the divine, the supernatural, the ethereal, it is not logical or credible – in fact it's outright dishonest – to claim an organization within atheism to relate in anyway with this definition. Only the usual suspects that prefer disorder to clarity will use the stratagem, thus securing through this cherry-picking process an association with the scientific method as "truth seekers", resulting in them possessing all the virtues and none of the flaws. In point of fact, this is nothing short of the equivocation fallacy they use in first place to deflect criticisms of the nature of the belief they hold. No matter how much denial the atheist immerses himself in he will still possess the inner thirst to adhere to some sort of institutional assembly he can find others who share the same common ground in terms of social conventions and practices.

FINGER POINTING

it's not me, it's you

The bishops of faux-atheism, the propagators of the message that you can adhere, or hold on to, values or principles designed by mainstream religions, often pretend to be people of reason. This appears to be the only avenue of luring their audience to join their flawed belief system. Further, they envisage a world full of critical thinking, of which they are part of – in fact they claim to be pioneers of such world, as they rid it of the addiction to religion. But what is this *critical thinking* process they speak of? The idea behind it is to form a judgment based on factual data and rational thought, in place of the preference and prejudice that are so often the downfall of human understanding. Inherently, it's intimately tied with the scientific method of pursuing the truth, where ideally one's opinion is kept to one's self, while facts are to be presented to everybody else.

But critical thinking starts at home, and atheists will have none of it, *faux* or not. The two equivocation fallacies mentioned previously established this, in particular the one that misrepresents atheism as neutral, or permitting it to appear so, while allowing the convenience of carrying a sword of battle to decapitate the theistic foe, eradicating the latter's absurd superstitious beliefs. Procuring the truth takes a backseat to antagonizing the opposition. Their speech may be full of grandiloquence, placing themselves on a pedestal of truth and virtue, but they always filter out the worst of their belief system has, only to embezzle the good things that aren't theirs. Were atheists free of the burden of faith and not possess the pressing need to attack and vilify the competing religions, they wouldn't need to resort to finger pointing, instead of actually engaging in critical thinking.

Let's look at one of the atheist's favorite topics when attempting to fulminate religious people: Creationism. There is indeed a broad spectrum of Christians that defend this theological argument, pointing out that the Bible mentions the world was created by God in six days "[...] And there was evening and there was morning, the sixth day." (Genesis 1:31); there is also those who propose that it could refer to six thousand years "[...] that with the Lord one day is like a thousand years, and a thousand years like one day." (2 Peter 3:8). Either of the arguments can be proven irredeemably false due to science demonstrating the Earth's age to be around 4.6 billion years old. The main issue here is of course interpretive, because atheists do not need to abide by the methodology of creationists and therefore they could accept the idea that the biblical verse could be read with a different meaning: the true value of text of the aforesaid verse from the book of Peter could be easily understood to signify that the passage of time is irrelevant to God, as He isn't bound by such constraint. Instead of engaging in the false rhetoric of finger pointing, bullying and harassing, the atheist could instead use his 'critical thinking' approach and educate those that lack such intellectual skill or will to see things this way out of comfort. Sadly, apparently it's the inverse and the atheist is the one that needs to be lectured and taught not to lie and distort, which they do repeatedly – after all they need to put that sword of battle to good use.

Another great example is that of the persistent attack on the Pentateuch, the first five books of the Bible that were written by Moses. Many of the prophets of *hateism* – the Holy Inquisitors of atheism that persecute religions tirelessly through their writings and speeches – adore extracting a verse from Genesis, Deuteronomy, or similar to point out how horrible the God of Christianity is: always selectively filtering the worst verses while avoiding the good ones altogether, as those will be put in the "It belongs to every religion" bucket. In fact, anything that is positive or has value that is in the Bible becomes public property, but the *bad* verses, the ones they disagree with, finger pointing it is. This is nothing more than a pejorative way of looking at religion – where is the critical thinking they promised?

The Bible is in truth one of the most wonderful books ever written, and as religious scripture it has a unique element to it, seeing it's not really a book as much as it is a collection of books, the entirety of it written across a time span of 1,700 years (without including oral tradition). This furnishes it with one of the most dramatic theological characteristics that one could find: it contains the evolution and the maturement of the people that worshiped the Biblical God in a way like no other religion offers. If the *hateist* were to be an objective, rational truth-seeker, not only he would have realized this but he would not be nitpicking on verses that are evidently obsolete and, in most circumstances, have been superseded by the latter books of the same compendium. The God of the Bible never changes, but we humans certainly do and, like a father with his own son, He adapted to the growing of His followers.

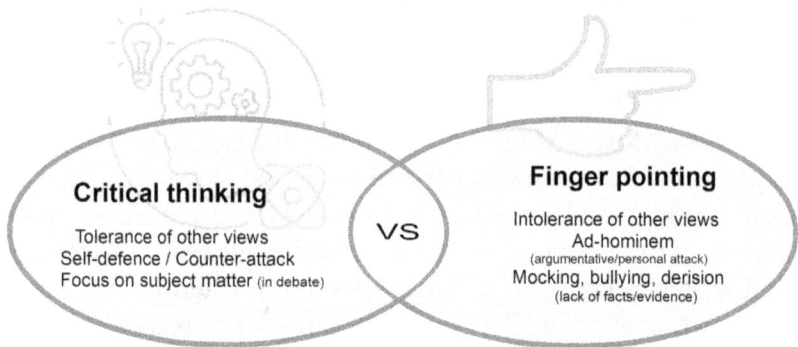

Figure 5: Critical thinking vs finger pointing

The misappropriation of all good things brought by religion by claiming they are *natural,* or "were just there", thereby removing all the merit from it, is nothing short of cheating. Only by attacking the objective flaws of religions, and not contemplating their own, including the lack of acceptance that atheism *is* a belief system, can they seduce others to join them, as per **Figure 5**. The lack of objectivity and rational process; the reliance on bad mouthing and ill intention; the accusatory stance, including derision and mockery; the request of, through panic mongering, the eradication of religion due to being the greatest cause of *harm* – whatever that word may mean under atheism, as a lot more pain, suffering and misery was committed under atheistic ideologies such as Communism and Nazism. All these correspond to the activity of finger pointing, *not* critical thinking as they falsely advertise.

PROPHETS OF HATRED

the unholy at war

The bishops of *hateism,* brandishing their sword of battle against the heretics – the ones who dare believe in an invisible, intangible God – often strive in fear mongering by spewing out doomsday conspiracies against them, such as the world could be in serious trouble if humans are to not rid themselves of religion. Only through banishing such deranged, fantasist practices can we achieve a safer society. They often bank on utilizing their confirmation bias to associate religion and the belief in God to acts of terrorism, cruelty or bigotry. They proselytize by claiming a lot of hatred would have disappeared from the world were we to turn to science and abandon religion. But one must ask: if religion were that dangerous, wouldn't the world have ended by now? After all religiosity was born thousands, potentially even tens of thousands, of years ago.

This anti-theist tirades leave a lot to be desired, although they are in their right to engage in them. One could add they have the *duty* of doing so, since anti-theism exists as a constitutive part of atheism, within the intrinsic act of animosity towards the enemy. If God does not exist and is purely fictional, what worth is there in wasting time with practices such as praying, worshiping or putting one's hopes on whatever might come in an afterlife that doesn't exist? If the atheist does not enter such crusade, he might as well join the ranks of another army, alongside the agnostic. This abundantly justifies the summoning of copious amounts of scorn and hatred from their camp.

But a serious problem arises: once inspecting the historic societal implementations of the atheistic doctrine, a death toll totaling over one hundred million people pops into view – and all in less than a century! They can disembarass themselves of this dark cloud easily through a few more sprinkles of *hateism* – just claim these regimes that caused this carnage to be religions, or religious groups, and throw them into the theistic side of the court. But this deceitful argument has been addressed previously as just another equivocation fallacy used by atheists. This endemic shadow over atheism cannot be made away with that easily by using such cheap trickery. If atheism gave rise to the doctrines of Socialism, Communism, Nazism and others, it must be accountable for their results. Claiming these to be related in any way to Christianity, Buddhism, Islam or any other true form of religious spiritual worship is not just preposterous but entirely pathetic and cowardly.

MISAPPROPRIATION

against the holy

As per usual, the prophets of hatred, who love disseminating fear through a lying rhetoric, misappropriate all good things brought by religion, as to detach their inherent value from their birthplace. Examples such as replacing A.D. (Anno Domini, which stands for *Year of our Lord*) and B.C. (Before Christ) with 'modern' entries that are accommodating to their narrative: CE (Common Era) and BCE (Before Common Era), which appear to be more inclusive to non-Christians. But if the year relates to exactly that, to the birth of Christ, why change the abbreviations? A non-follower of Christ is still using a representation created by Christians, which was then exported across the four corners of the globe, making it the world-wide calendar system. If the era is 'common', it's solely because it is following a date system based on the Biblical text, hence it being named *Gregorian calendar* – there is nothing else 'common' about it. The strategy, were it pure in its intention, could have even kept the same acronym but use the appropriate designations of Christian Era (for CE) and Before Christian Era (BCE) and it would have rid of the problem of 'Our Lord' not being befitting to be used by people that aren't Christian. But the intentions were hardly pure of heart, instead reflecting the true need to take away the value of the modern calendar from being based on the birth of the Christian Messiah, and pretending it's an era 'common' to everyone across the world.

Another good example is the Golden Rule, which has been turned into a *global* tenet, as a moral postulate invented by humans, while in fact – in it's directive and positive form at least – can be sourced in an inalienably from the gospel in the Bible "And just as you want people to treat you, treat them in the same way." (Luke 6:31), directly quoting Jesus of Nazareth. Now it's unequivocally true other religions carried the same message, even though often in a prohibitive, thence self-serving form – *don't hurt me and I won't hurt you* sort of affair. Irrespective of which religions carry the most merits in this regard, shouldn't the atheist question the validity of such standard when being skeptical of the gods that provided their followers with it? Just agreeing with such rule out of preference is nothing short of weak and irrational, putting atheists' credibility into question.

One could add other items to the list aplenty, but suffice to say the averment, from the atheist camp, that these and many other tenets or concepts are *natural* – thereby reverting all merits that any religions and whichever gods they revere, while at the same time placing focus on their poor outcomes and direct attention on their flaws – is incongruent, malicious and downright dishonest.

THE SALES PITCH

elixir of soot

Humans can use science to predict, with fair accuracy, a lot of physical phenomena based on *cause-and-effect*. The fact that the universe depends on things happening as a result of something else, i.e. there must always be a catalyst based on universal laws that brings about a reaction, allows us to foretell events within a limited capacity, like, for instance, the sunrise and sunset. The philosophical theory of *determinism* originates from this knowledge, drawing the conclusion that everything is subjugated by the universe's causality narrative. The slippery slope into meaninglessness is unavoidable, quickly reaching the logical sequitur: nothing is forbidden, everything is permitted. However, the faux-atheists' appetite is not in tune with this idiom, using preference or opinion as an override that 'fixes' the problem.

Enter *compatibilism*, the philosophical theory that relies on an individual's motivation to turn him into an agent, thus making him accountable for his actions and decisions. The *motive* itself is predetermined, following the deterministic rules of cause-and-effect, but the individual's *freewill* results in inference of liability. The absurdity of the whole notion is immediately apparent due to the brain of such individual being subject in its entirety to the same laws of the natural world that govern everything else, i.e. the activity of the brain – usually referred to as the *mind* by the atheist – exist equally under cause-and-effect, no more, no less. In fact, one wouldn't need a magnifying lens to realize compatibilism is nothing short of a reversion back to Christianity and its deep-rooted values and principles, in a desperate attempt to slide all the way down the slope (**Figure 6**). They created a monster and now frantically seek to flee from it. In effect, the theory of compatibilism can be seen as a Frankenstein with lipstick: faux-atheists created their own abomination, where freedom of will is concerned, and once they saw how ugly it was, they applied some make-up to it – but the result is the monster is still visibly hideous.

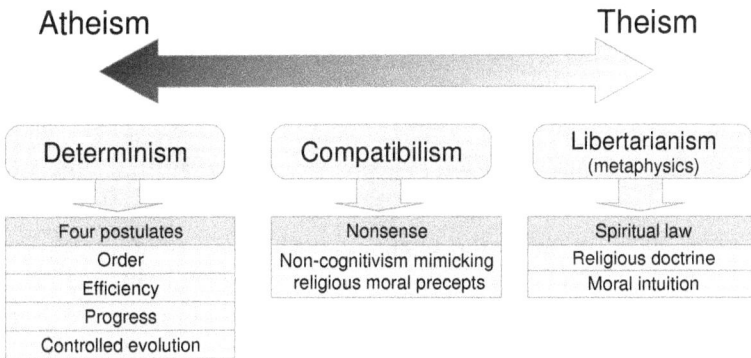

Determinism	Compatibilism	Libertarianism (metaphysics)
Four postulates	Nonsense	Spiritual law
Order	Non-cognitivism mimicking religious moral precepts	Religious doctrine
Efficiency		Moral intuition
Progress		
Controlled evolution		

Figure 6: Atheists fear their own creation

Metaphysical libertarianism, also known as *libertarian free will*, depends on a duality of the *body* and *mind*, where the latter must exist in an insubstantial form, therefore belonging to the metaphysical domain. This prospect is too appealing to the faux-atheist, as it caters for the autonomy of the human being, because it irredeemably nullifies the reductive prospect of being nothing more than a clump of cells, operating under absolute compliance to the laws of physics – exactly what determinism has to offer. Since agency is no more, the snake oil salesmen raise the bottle up high and offer it to the audience: what's in the bottle; what mysterious substance does it contain? "Try it! It will heal all ailments!", they say, compelling one to fall into the fallacious, deceptive net filled with wonderful and magical properties. Disappointingly, there's no elixir of youth, only a concoction designed to circumvent the ugly truth any faux-atheist is forced to embrace: compatibilism is nothing more than the fool's gold.

Not much due diligence is needed to see through the shadiness: if they talk the talk, make them walk the walk. They fraudulently point in one direction, then walk towards another, in a fast stride. In all practicality, the faux-atheist, or any form of atheist for that matter, should follow four postulates: *Order, Progress, Efficiency* and *Controlled evolution*. The first two are widely familiar to the atheist cause, with *efficiency* being brought over from what we can observe in the animal kingdom to achieve best results. And finally *controlled evolution*, as humans far supplanted the need to sit and wait for nature to do its business. From stem cell research, prosthetic limbs, pace-makers, cybernetic implants and so much more have been achieved in the last few decades of human history. Who needs nature to tell you what to do when you can choose to be on the driving seat? But instead, the faux-atheist diverts its strategy to a fatalistic approach of claiming that it is simply "The way we are", when in all other cases, most surely when getting rid of God, the very same plan of action does not apply from their end.

FATALISM

one bundle to rule them all

The art of deceiving encompasses changing gears when necessary, and that is exactly what faux-atheists do. If they present themselves as being on the driving seat when disposing of religion and its practices, throwing them into the bottomless pit of all things obsolete and archaic, they quickly shift into a fatalistic posture when dealing with morality, freewill, love, the meaning of life, existential dread and more. The latter must be kept around, or so they say, as these are presented as necessary for human accomplishment – even survival, perhaps. The claims are never justified, just asserted in a clearly dogmatic narrative. But one must open his eyes and see things for what they are: if the faux-atheist deprecates God and afterlife, along with everything these ethereal matters forcibly encapsulate, they must also bring the aforementioned elements for consideration. Which they sadly don't, instead concocting a web of comforting lies so they can avoid inconvenient truths.

Hateism discards religion as something useless and fantasist, while keeping everything else that would (and must) also fall into those categories. This follows the patterns of 'disproving' the existence of God, or bringing forward information that would lead to such proclivity, using confirmation bias while affirming the necessity of *well-being* (by way of humanism), freewill (through compatibilism) and others. All to reinforce the need to justify the value of the individual by means of motivated reasoning. If the faux-atheist *wants* something to be kept, let any inconvenient truths not pose an obstacle and instead retrofit explanations that will mask the fact their preference was at the helm of the argument.

If God is nothing more than mere fantasy of those who find solace in belonging to something greater then a cold, callous universe, then all other things that cannot be made certain through the laws of nature should follow the same path. If religion is the opium of the masses, so is morality, freewill, love, compassion, altruism, the meaning of life, the value of the individual, good and evil. At the end of the day, and according to real atheism, we are nothing more than rational machines that should focus on the four postulates of atheism, this manner ridding ourselves of any drugs that may get in the way.

Bowing to faux-atheism is self-defeating, as it renders us humans as junkies in need of a fix. Some will resort to worship of God, so they believe their actions will have a reward after they depart, while hoping to reach heaven; others will procure to behave morality to *feel* good by doing the *right* thing (whatever that may be); others will engage in loving relationships as a form of decorating their lives with fancy motifs. What is not acceptable is for the faux-atheist to recur to logic and reason to express sympathy towards some of the *drugs,* while displaying antipathy towards the rest. If humans are to keep these drugs, so be they keep them all as a full package. Either overdose on any of the soothing, imaginary filters we use to distract ourselves from the ugly truth, or throw them all away. The deal must be so that either all go, or they all stay.

CHAPTER 3

The Amoral Code

THE FALSE DILEMMA FALLACY

a sinuous path

One of the key arguments faux-atheists utilize to defend the preservation of a moral landscape within societies is the false idea that if we discard these values altogether, we would be left with a free-for-all approach where crime would be rampant and, eventually and inevitably, humans would end up all killing each other. Nothing could be further from the truth as there are other options available that could represent civilizational growth and success without the said moral values and ethical principles. According to these atheists, morality is 'innate' to humans but can't the same be said about God? Has any group of humans been found to exist without any sense of divine worship, even if directing it to human leaders, animals or celestial bodies? If a society were to turn to other options, such as order and progress, it could indeed achieve results without these false dilemma of claiming we either keep a moral code of conduct, or unavoidably will club each other to death.

An hypothetically *robotized* society can be used to

disprove the need for morals. Like it is often seen in science-fiction movies, the suggestion that if a world made of androids were to exist, would they all necessarily exterminate each other? Seems quite the contrary, as the way this type of fiction addresses the issue pends towards the idea that they would focus on efficiency and evolution. Even if they were to be seen as a threat to humanity, were we to build such advanced electronic entities, it would be most likely solely due to considering themselves a superior life-form, hence the need to eradicate the endemic threat that humans would constitute to their own civilization. This would not be seen through an emotional lens, nor a moral one, but instead under the fair reasoning of which group is more worthy of being graced with survival out of rational superiority. Which lifeform would be more suitable to explore, discover and progress in a more expeditious fashion.

To attest morality as needless, an example can be brought up. On an intersection with fully functioning traffic lights, a driver of a vehicle proceeds to rush through the intersection in a perilous manner blatantly ignoring a red light. As a consequence he causes a high-speed collision with another car that simply obeyed the rules, as the light was green for its passengers. If the collision ends up leading to the death of the passengers of the vehicle that did not commit the infraction, one could state that it's morally unacceptable due to tragic deaths involved – especially if the passengers of the obeying vehicle were vulnerable people such as a mother and a child, added just for dramatic effect. In reality morality has nothing to do with it, since the violation of the rules, were it to lead to many deaths or none at all, would still comprise significant upset to others traveling through the intersection. This without mentioning the costs and logistics of removal of debris and other damage, plus costs associated with the repairing of the vehicles.

In fact, placing the same occurrence in a world where only androids (droids designed in humanoid form) exist, and assuming they would have built roads and traffic light systems similar to our own, would lead to the same results. Even if in the case one of the androids traveling in its vehicle through the intersection were to be damaged by the accident, it could easily be repaired, or even fully replaced, without any moral implications. It's simply an inefficient way to design a societal model, since a traffic congestion would still take place, the costs of repair would still be present, and the emergency services would still be called to deal with the whole unnecessary ordeal, to put out fires or remove debris, and so on and so forth.

A world of androids would still require order and rules for the need to avoid inefficiency, self-mutilation, damage or destruction. There is no need for morals or an ethos for such a world, because it would function perfectly without any feelings, thereby exposing the fake argument that the main problem with a car crash is of moral nature at all – reason alone can provide a solution without resorting to a moral layer placed on top of it, discarding any need for any moral conduct whatsoever. The moral argument is nothing but a ruse to attempt to excuse the idea of maintaining something so redundant and impractical, because such values, more often than not, get in the way of efficiently coming up with a blueprint for a successful society. Indeed, the android world model is but an option out of many.

If moral *good* and *evil* are subjective, an amoral code could take place that would allow all – nothing is forbidden, everything is permitted. No overseer or observer, hence humans do as they will. An *Hitlerian* system, i.e. a world where humanity had been subject to the conquest of the *Third Reich* at global scale, would see itself freed from war and many other social hindrances and time-wasting activities. The group of the few considered superior would enslave the remaining billions under military control and surveillance from the secret services, forestalling any insurrections and conspiracies. Moreover the elites would be served by the pleb, who would bend over backwards simply to survive, with their offspring often being used a currency, as they could provide their rulers with sexual pleasures or esclavagist servitude. The elites, in their superiority, would revel not only in luxuries and pleasures, but would also be freed of chores and cumbersome tasks, as maids, chauffeurs, body guards, mechanics, builders, etc. would be widely available at no cost. These superior peoples could then dedicate themselves to improve society and augment human civilization with technological breakthroughs and scientific advancements. By now, humanity would have probably been able to fully colonize planet Mars, establishing it as a stepping stone into interstellar space travel.

But the faux-atheist will suddenly worry about the slaves *well-being*, therefore making justice to the addition of the prefix *faux* to their belief system. The question is, why prioritize happiness, something that has been reduced to chemicals in the brain by their own accord, instead of progress and efficiency? Wasting millions of hours taking selfies, partying, drinking, dancing, romancing, watching sports or reality television shows, marching, rioting, protesting, plus many other frivolous endeavors most humans devote their entire lives to. Without doubt these wasteful activities are certainly some of the things that a society existing under such a militaristic model would rid itself off entirely, leaving any feelings or emotional complaints in the dirt. But, as per usual, the faux-atheist talks the talk but does not show any intention of walking the walk.

METAETHICS

by law or by choice?

If morality can be defined as something endogenous to the human mind, where the desire to be *good* determines how an action is taken, ethics can be seen as a system of moral conduct engineered by those who perceive their moral setup to be correct. A social *ethos* is built based on these doctrines, the study of which we refer to as *normative ethics* – or what a particular society perceives as good or evil. The ontological element however, the subject of the *nature* of ethics and how they came to be, is the object of study of the philosophical and psychological field of *metaethics*. Even when trying to dig deep into these matters, it's possible for one to become quickly aware that there are only two distinct sources where moral doctrines can possibly originate from. One is the objective source that requires cognition, thus being attributed the logical name *cognitivism,* the other a subjective source referred to appropriately as *non-cognitivism.*

Both of these theoretical moral frameworks can themselves be broken into two moral theories (as can be found on **Figure 7**): *naturalism* and *intuitivism* for the former, where *good* and *evil* are exogenous to the human mind and understood as laws that exist regardless of human appreciation; for the latter *emotivism* and *prescriptivism,* which originate from a society's conscious collective absolutes that are created through agreement, usually under majority rule.

If cognitivism relies on an absolute set of laws humans cannot control but instead only embrace and potentially harness, the same cannot be said for its counterpart, where the maxim of *nothing is forbidden, everything is permitted* haunts any attempts of making sense of *which* moral recipe to choose from. Without an overseer or observer, without an eye in the sky watching what we do and will, we are free to roam the Earth guiding each culture under moral relativism, where no boundaries nor global behavioral standards can be made to make sense, resulting in a great moral divide.

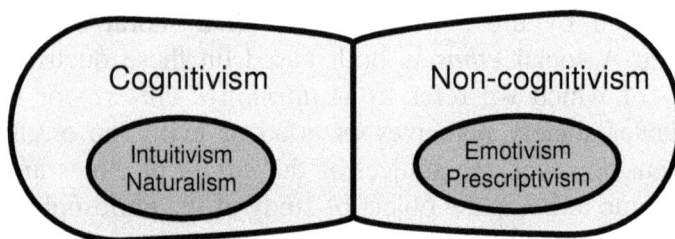

Figure 7: The two paths of metaethics

ETHICAL NATURALISM

nothing without the spirit

If one were to seek for a set of ethical norms from within the physical universe, the laws of nature would certainly turn out to be a major obstacle to overcome. There is nothing ethical or moral about the rules that regulate wildlife other than *eugenics*, i.e. the survival of the fittest. The stronger, whether physically, agilely or intellectually, will dominate the frail and the weak. However, due to the intrinsic need of faux-atheists to use motivated reasoning so they can retrofit empirical data as a means to justify things they chose to preserve, such as a moral landscape, they are made to obsess in the search of a potential solution for their conundrum. Under *ethical naturalism*, all features that compose the natural world can be used to settle arguments regarding the need for certain human practices and behavioral instructions. Pain, pleasure, cooperation and other objective experiences can be the foundation to a multitude of ethical theories, such as humanism, consequentialism and utilitarianism, all of which are intimately tied to *material reductionism*. The latter is the philosophical idea that reduces all complex things to simpler, less complex parts of the material universe, thereby allowing everything that there is to be interpreted through the study of the smallest of particles, genes, molecules, DNA, etc.

The neuroscientist Sam Harris approached the issue of the faux-atheist moral conundrum by using a stove analogy. The idea is if a person does not wish to have their hand on a hot stove, this can be perceived as a breach of the individual's *well-being* and therefore be classified as *evil*. As simplistic approach as this may be, it decorates their ethos with the required ingredients to make it work. Or does it? Here's a deconstruction of the argument, assuming the end result to be exactly identical regardless of each scenario presented:

- If the individual places the hand on the hot stove himself, this action is <u>not</u> perceived as evil.
- If the individual accidentally touched the hot stove, it's <u>not</u> perceived as evil.

- If someone forced the individual's hand to touch the hot stove, it <u>is</u> perceived as evil.

This exposes the fallacy involved in the argument, where pain leads to moral values. The fact is that only in one of the cases above (the interfering third-party's action) would be considered evil from a moral perspective, as in both other cases any sort of agency was absent. Firstly, if an accident took place, it cannot be classified as evil unless we are to blame every random phenomena that occurs repeatedly for many of the evils of the world; secondly, if the actor was the one inflicting pain on himself deliberately, making it falling short of being considered evil – masochistic perhaps, but certainly no immorality involved in the act. The idea of pain as a metric to define moral paradigms doesn't work, and neither do any of the other experiences our body, in its multiple interactions with the world, can supply us with. This type of *scientism* (the devotion of one-self to science, nearing the point of zealous worship) can never reach a universal conclusion, because any information gathered from the natural world offers too many limitations to explain the human moral code – irrespective of culture, traditions and creed.

Pain itself cannot therefore be used as a causal argument to define *evil*, as only seldom there is a correlation between the two. On closer inspection, it's actually possible to verify that pain can be understood as an *is*, whereas the immoral action that leads to pain, what one would call *evil* and thus falling in the immoral spectrum, belongs to the *ought* category. Since pain only exists due to the brain being signaled a warning when damage is inflicted to one's body, this is not a subjective matter but rather an objective one, as it sprung from nature creating living organisms with an inbuilt system to ensure their safeguarding. Take the case of a paraplegic: if one were to hammer his leg violently, the body would still incur the damage but the brain would not be signaled anything, so no *pain* would be perceived by the victim – does this not qualify as evil? Same could be said in respect to someone in a coma, under heavy sedation, etc. The damage to the body will always occur, because even when the mechanism that our body uses to alert the brain of danger is broken, the universe still operates under the same laws. As such, *pain* itself is objective but the evil deed can happen without any pain being involved, proving the two independent.

Furthermore, the hot stove argument is preceded with circular logic, where the well-being of the actor seems to have a magical value attributed to it. What is this concept of being well in first place? Why would one regarding other people's suffering if he himself wouldn't be subject to such pain? Would it not be beneficial to allow others to have their hands placed in the hot stove in order to save our own? It seems the world is filled with constructs, such as the hero archetype that requires one to sacrifice his own *well-being* for the sake of others, completely contradicting the previously established logic. Indeed, most values ascribed to humanism and other ethical theories are often plagiarized from Christian values and dogma. They start by *preferring* a set of values and only then attempting to justify them with 'scientific' and 'rational' explanations. The values are not extracted from experience, but instead they are preemptively selected as necessary, and a poorly manufactured theory soon follows to fill in the blanks. The big question is: why have morality at all? Why not build an amoral society based on other tenets, such as order and efficiency? Morality should at least be reasoned as *not* innate. People move forward because of technology and, eventually, the previously suggested robotized world would work with no need for morals or ethics. The fatalist view that a human is but a mere function of the universe, a machine without meaning, nothing but a pile of stardust, cannot be dismissed nor ignored.

As pain itself cannot be constituted as the source of evil, the judgment on the action is the differential, which can be easily flipped on its head if justifiable: what if it's a murderer's hand being placed on the stove? Even when a third-party is implicated in the scenario, the action can still be considered *good*. But who is the murderer going to kill? What if he is going to assassinate the new Hitler? And is the action of murdering bad? Where does this definition come from? The moral vacuum that atheists live in can only be fulfilled when resorting to this sort of dogma that is presented as scientific endeavor when it actually isn't. They hopelessly and haplessly find refuge in defending Christian values that are established, and seen as intrinsic to the society they inhabit, making it impossible to detach from them. Asserting morality is *good*, when the idea of good in itself requires morality is begging the question which can only be 'fixed' with the aforementioned atheistic dogma, frequently referred to as *moral duty* – but where does the *duty* come from? All there is left is *Agrippa's Trilemma*, covered later in this book.

PREFERABLE BEHAVIOR

categorical imperatives revisited

With the lack of a scientific answers, embracing belief is always the shortest route to success. The Canadian author of Universally Preferable Behavior (UPB) Stefan Molyneux brought up a supposedly outstanding achievement in the field of ethics, resolving what philosophers for thousand of years had been unable to do so. According to himself, he found a set of *preferable* rules that, being universal, could be accepted as objectively necessary for the functioning of human society. If this idea sounds familiar it's because it is: the German philosopher Immanuel Kant (1724 – 1804 A.D.) came up with a similar concept centuries before, although without the proclamation of any sort of feat. The Kantian Categorical Imperatives are based on the same concept of *universality principle*, forming the essence of this philosopher's deontology. A whole plethora of maxims is offered that must be abided to, under any and all circumstances. *Do Y* in any given situation has been proven to not be worthy of pursuing, as it often leads to conflicting results, as stated in the hot stove example in the previous section.

Taking as an example where a pregnant woman breaks water at a fuel station, turning the affair into an emergency in terms of taking her to the nearby hospital as soon as possible. The only positive outcome comes from 'borrowing' (stealing as it would be without permission) an expensive car its wealthy owner left near the pump while going to pay for the fuel. The way the situation was staged makes it appear there is legitimacy in theft, even though that would be perceived as an *is* under Molyneux's doctrine. Even if the car ended up being returned, what if damaged had been made to the car in the haste of reaching the medical service? Not to mention the likely mess left in the back sit where the pregnant lady would have sat, or the disruption this could have caused the wealthy car owner – maybe whatever affairs he had that moment were more significant to humanity than the pregnant woman's health or her baby's.

The UPB is also riddled with conflations of *is* and *ought*, as per **Figure 8**, where often objective facts are presented as moral questions, thence leading to the false sense of reaching some sort of resolution when it comes to *Hume's law:* there is no *ought* from an *is*. In fact, Kantian Categorical Imperatives are used in conjunction with consequentialist views to provide an hybrid solution of sorts. Moral values become objective out of the value they bring into society, therefore being accepted as necessities rather than preferences. With some minor variations, the same flaws present in the 18th century German philosopher's deontology is also witnessed in Molyneux's, with the obvious incongruities and inconsistencies making their appearance. And this conclusion is reached without even addressing many of the flaws in the Canadian's author ability to use syllogistic logic without the pitfalls of the highly atheist-friendly circular and dogmatic arguments.

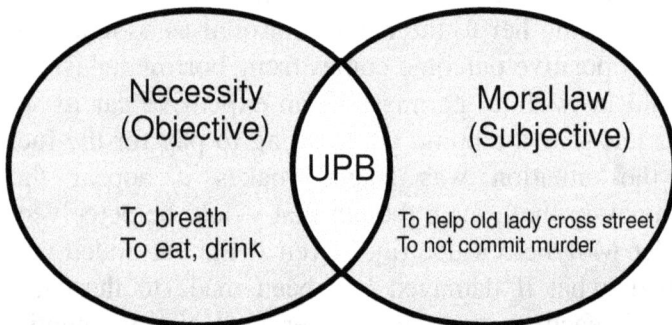

Figure 8: UPB conflates *ought* with *is*.

The main problem with these models is the idea of the *ought* being endogenous to the mind, whereas the *is* can be proven to be exogenous to it, leaving no space for a final determination, one that would be without doubt or conflict. If morality is subjective, it becomes fully prescriptive, allowing for moral relativism, including that of a fully amoral model, and preferable behavior is thus not universal but local to each culture or creed. There is no true *right* or *wrong*, *good* or *evil* – an atheistic moral landscape where once more nothing is forbidden, everything is permitted is the only absolute truth. Exclusively when both the *ought* and the *is* are predicated in objectivity can the issue be truly solved.

THE CONCEALED ASYMMETRY

parting of the waters

One of the tricks played very often by faux-athcists in order to justify their moral values, whether through naturalism or any other ethical setup, is to present rational arguments as being moral. The most obvious example is using the field of medicine to refer to *well-being*. In truth it relates to efficiency, since well performed medical procedures are in tune with human views of what is morally good, thence the conflation. This gimmick is just a means of concealing the fact there are two distinct fields that need to be interpreted, each of which can be seen as a vector, or an arrow, with independent directions (**Figure 9**).

As an example, if a blind old woman was waiting to cross the street and needed the aid of a passerby to do so, should the latter help the disabled individual, even if that would cause the passerby to miss an important job interview that would land him the career of his dreams? To add insult to injury, what if that career would down the road bless the world with an invention that would change humanity forever – is it still noble for the man to miss that interview to help a useless, impaired old lady? Trying to rationalize morality leads to the clear conflict of what is (rationally) *correct* and *incorrect,* and what is (morally) *right* and *wrong.* The honest atheist will descend into the realm of eugenics, dysgenics, utilitarianism, post-modernism, post-structuralism (all of which are discussed in detail in later chapters) or any other formulas that remove such hindrance. Subsequently, morality is either thrown-out altogether or demoted to an opinion out of convenience of any particular group that benefits from it. A differentiation must be made from the rational *Good vs Bad,* or correct and incorrect, and the moral *Good vs Evil,* or right and wrong.

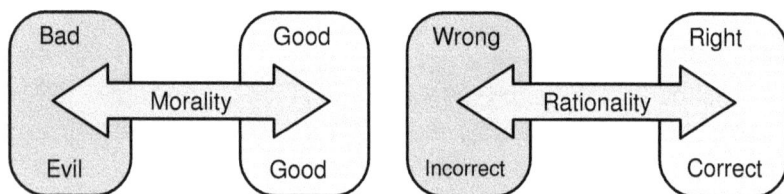

Figure 9: The vectors of morality and rationality

Returning to the previous example, it would be not only correct for the passerby to neglect helping the disabled old lady, but it would also make sense for him to bump into to her if that aided him catching the bus in order to land the job. If humanity would benefit immensely from this option, then this should be the route to take, whereas whatever the consequences suffered by the disabled old lady – even in the drastic eventuality of the bump leading her to fall onto the road and get hit by a car – are of little to no relevance to society. In this example, the vector of rationality would be pointing towards *good* if the passerby were to bump into the old lady (as this would be the *correct* path, seeing it would lead to advantageous results to the whole of humanity). Conversely the action would be perceived as *evil* (as his behavior would be morally wrong, due to selfishness, disrespect and even negligence towards a weak, vulnerable person) by anyone observing the occurrence or learning about the incident. This conundrum isn't solvable, as these two vectors don't resemble any indication of belonging to the same set of laws, and instead are entirely separate fields.

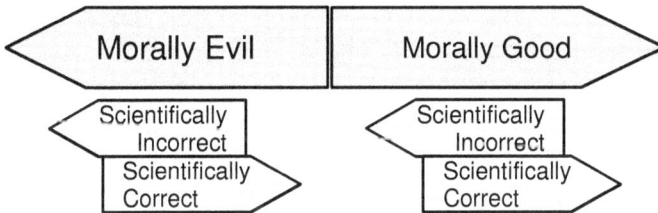

Figure 10: The juxtaposition of morality and rationality

However, these asymmetries can be made confusing, resorting to arguments as the aforementioned medicine and the encompassing *well-being*, as in all cultures it would be fair to presume it's universal to associate medical scientific achievements with moral good. Healing people and saving lives is always welcome from a spiritual point of view, where human life is seen as having inherent value as opposed to being a commodity for the benefit of the whole – or the illustrious others. The Hippocratic Oath, which can be can summarized as "Do no harm", is still taken to this day in all medical careers, making the moral argument prevail over particular social interests, such as when healing a violent career criminal. This leads to the illusion that an objective answer has been found when defining moral values under the guise of searching for *well-being*, when this illusive concept is itself undermined by the preferences of happiness, prosperity and joy, which in turn are illusory themselves. To avoid this perpetual "moving of the goalposts", it's best to look into examples outside medicine, as it's the most misleading science to use. In short, due to the nature of the specific scientific field of medicine, the vectors of morality and rationality are aligned the vast majority of the time, making them almost indistinguishable.

Furthermore, when addressing human moral behavior, it's assumed a father will still jump in front of the car to save his child, whereas in the wild kingdom it would most likely function otherwise. But it must be asked: why develop strategies that are contrary to the laws of the jungle, and how were we to deviate to such an extent from such laws, when our success as a species far surpasses any other? Yet we are tied to such absurd beliefs that originated from our intrinsic need to worship imaginary, invisible supreme deities. The argument could be presented that humans needed moral laws for a certain period of time, so we could cooperate and benefit from strength in numbers during our specie's early days. But is there still any need to keep the same rules of old, now that we are the dominant species on the planet and colonized every corner of the globe, transforming it into safe human habitats? No other species pose a threat any longer, and little can the elements do to hurt us, aside from the odd, situational cataclysm, we are in full control of our destiny – or we will be once we throw the *arrow* of morality out the window and speed towards transhumanism, utilitarianism or any non-feelings, non-preferences dependent ethos. Instead, faux-atheists persist on juggling excuses, one after the other, to keep ethical norms 'manufactured' by religions and their made-up gods.

HIERARCHY OF VALUES

man shall not live of bread alone

The pyramid of moral values can refer to socio-economics, religion and human necessities, with a value hierarchy comprising a chain of values in relation to each other. The main problem arises when these values bifurcate and become incompatible – it's soon apparent there isn't *one* hierarchy of values, but *two* hierarchies. Looking at insects as an example, it's possible to determine these only have care for their survival and the group they're inserted in, if any. They need to feed, reproduce, build their nests and defend them. Thus, they follow a single hierarchy of values that relate to their own survival in a harsh world. This can be defined as the hierarchy of *is* values, i.e. the values that are driven out of *necessity*, as these are the ones bound by the laws of nature and the universe. These creatures do not have any moral needs or spiritual ones, turning their continuance into a simple mechanical affair – either survive and strive, or perish in a ruthless, competing world.

Human beings are quite different, as their needs far surpass the need to eat, sleep and procreate. Our species requires the fulfillment of hope and dreams, of reaching goals and acquiring greater self-awareness and understanding of who we are, and especially *why* we are. This forces us into the second hierarchy of values, i.e. the *ought* values that are driven out of *meaning* (**Figure 11**). A human life is more than that of a machine-like entity like the previously mentioned inferior lifeforms. Humans not only procure to reason how the universe works but also why it exists at all, a question that clearly transcends the laws of physics. We need the light at the end of the tunnel, the hope that we will reach a higher state of existence – the incessant search for God as the existential axiom. Insects, reptiles, fish, birds and any mammals except ourselves do not worry about such dealings, their lives and duties being fully circumscribed to this fishbowl we call the universe and its integral laws.

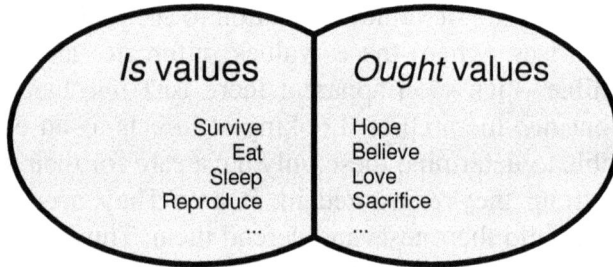

Figure 11: Is/Ought values hierarchies

Morality is thus an excellent means of proving we see more than the laws of physics permit. We see the *ought* that cannot be attached to, nor originate from, an *is*. Pain can result in rage, sadness, sorrow, depression, unhappiness, suffering and any other negative emotional states, but cannot be the cause of evil, since there's simply the occasional correlation between the two. In fact pain can be described as an *is*, whereas evil as an *ought*.

When there is a convergence of both, whether under a positive or negative prism, confusion can set in and the idea that only one hierarchy of values is required can appear as a logical solution. But when such values are divergent, that is when one is positive and the other is negative, the atheistic game is up and the truth is brought into light. Humans cannot derive their behavior solely from an hierarchy of *is* values like many inferior creatures do – indeed we require a hierarchy of *ought* values to function beyond the barrenness and sterility of a mechanistic state of being.

MORAL RELATIVISM

better is worse, worse is better

The definition of the word *moral* has a dual meaning, both referring to the general concept itself but also when performing a positive moral action. *Positive morality* is then identified with a good deed and, conversely, *negative morality* is when engaging in an immoral action. If amorality is the rejection of any moral laws, thereby legitimizing any human act as not having any moral implications, immorality is still embedded in the moral framework of any culture, consisting of what opposes the positive aspects of morality. Even though this base notion is shared among all societies and cultures, making it an absolute requirement for any moral construct, *what* constitutes positive or negative actions can vary across the social groups, making moral prescriptions relative to each society and fully dependent on its religion, traditions, habits, etc.

There is a common ground between societies in respect to certain practices that tend to be generally seen as positive, such as charity, and others as negative, such as murder. Nonetheless, the real question relates to the perception of the predicament any moral landscape is under: is morality to be understood as objective or subjective? This constitutes a portion of the subject of study of the philosophical field known as *metaethics*, with strict, direct consequences to its child field *normative ethics*, which in turn studies the impact of ethical actions within a social model, i.e. the wrongness or righteousness of any particular form of human behavior. Any of these models will contain their own restrictions on what its constituents can and cannot do – what is defined as *the law* – but less often is the fear of punishment put into question, were one to violate said laws. It's logical to not commit murder if that leads someone to spend a lifetime in prison as consequence, but would one kill another were they given the guarantee to be able do so without any repercussions within the next ten minutes?

Atheists, due to rejection of any metaphysical laws, either adopt the prescriptive formula where the societal ethos is created through agreement and convenience, or the naturalistic formula where there is an attempt to extract ethical norms from the natural environment humans reside in and depend on. Nonetheless, it's quite easy to deconstruct both of these approaches as logic and reason can be used to demonstrate their flaws and inadequacies. One could bring forth an example with two islands, both of which with a limited number of inhabitants, and supposing these islands to be completely isolated from the rest of the world as well from each other – they know and communicate with no one. Each island, unbeknownst to them, has identical rules in terms of their population management and they only allow one-hundred adults to be alive at any given time, fifty belonging to the prime generation, fifty to the elderly one. Adding to this, they can only have fifty children, which will comprise the youth generation at any given time, until it matures and replaces the prime generation, which now has in turn replaced the elderly one. For the sake of simplicity, each of these generations has exactly fifty percent of females and males so they can easily pair with one another for reproductive reasons. The outcome is, there are never more than one-hundred and fifty people at a given time in either island, allowing resources not to be exhausted as they are limited. Violating these rules at any moment will lead to overpopulation, drought, famine, social upheaval and ensuing civilizational collapse. The only difference between each island (hence the need for two) is that one follows prescribed moral values while the other is wholly amoral. All their inhabitants are atheistic for simplicity's sake.

Both societies on each island strive equally until one day multiple cases of sterility occur concurrently, affecting the youth generations. Most of the twenty-five young females from each island are born without the ability to produce egg cells, leading to the obvious assumption that this will be the end of the road for both civilizations. Or maybe not so, as the inhabitants of the island that adopted amorality can simply kill their female younglings without any repercussions, as they only value life in terms of how efficient and invaluable it is to their own survival – they are truly eusocial and follow its doctrine in all respects, including the premise of valuing the health of their society over that of the individual, making utilitarian principles widely accepted. Constrastingly, the other island is now in a conundrum where, due to their moral prescriptions which include prohibiting any type of murder, they are forced to keep the useless female generation alive and have more babies in the hope these are not only mostly of the female gender, but they would not suffer from the same epidemic (refer to **Figure 12**). Either way, sooner or later this will certainly lead to their demise due to the breach of their most important rule against overpopulation, leaving as the only alternative the moral collapse of such society where, like in the other island, amorality would reign supreme. A faux-atheist could clumsily suggest that because the entire population's survival is at stake, the murder of the female youths would be an act of self-defense, but were one to be informed this situation actually occurs anywhere in the world, would it not lead to condemnation? Despite any gimmicks being brought over to hide the problem, the conclusion is still quite visible, relenting on the idea that murder is necessary, and cannot be strictly prohibited under a prescribed or naturalistic ethos, ending in the logical conclusion that morality is relative to each group's needs.

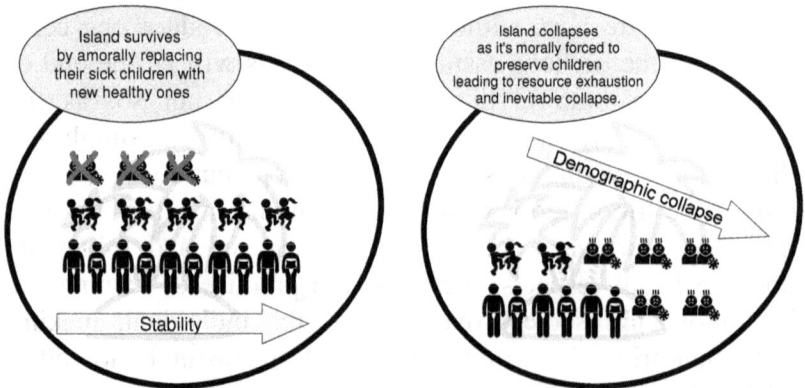

Figure 12: A clear example where morality conflicts with rationality

Moral altruism (humanistic definition for when actions taken are not necessarily advantageous to the benefactors engaging in them) could be brought into the equation, but the results would not diverge and the islanders would go extinct regardless of naming conventions. *Moral duty* could be actioned by the struggling tribe, but moral relativism would ensue, and murdering for different causes or reasons would soon gain support – if one excuse can be used to kill, so can many.

MORAL OBJECTIVISM

a gift from God

Ordinarily morality is implied as being a trait exclusive to humans, leaving animals to engage in what can be interpreted to as *ethical egoism*, where the self-interest of an agent legitimizes its actions and behavior. In the wild kingdom there is overwhelming dominance of the animal side in neglect of the spirit, effectively resulting in the *survival of the fittest*, also known as the law of the jungle. The smarter, faster, most efficient killers live off the weaker, less intelligent ones. Nature sorts itself out in a hierarchy of eugenics, where the superior rule and consume the inferior. This is the main reason most herbivores, with the exception of a few of the large pachyderm, live in herds and reproduce in great numbers, ensuring the aliveness of their species.

Yet, there are astounding examples in the wild where wild beasts seem to react to something more than their basic instinct for survival, at least when it comes to the class of animals known as mammals. In a wildlife documentary, a herd of African elephants is shown migrating, only to stop in order to caress the bones of a deceased juvenile member of their species, and doing so in a ritualistic and profoundly affectionate manner, contrasting extensively with their pressing need to escape the drought. Even if this behavior is only displayed for a few minutes, it still negates them the effectiveness of their migratory pattern: to find a region that contains water in abundance to ensure the subsistence of the herd. Moreover, this appears to be clearly a religious act, like that of valuing a bone structure that should be seen as nothing more than a defunct member of their species, if not just a pile of bones without any meaning. It's as if they read *value* where there was none, at least from a perspective of reason. But if these beasts are indeed conscious, if they are self-aware to the point they understand the *meaning* of the skeleton lies on the identity, along with all its idiosyncratic traits which that unique lifeform once carried within it (its soul), then it's very much likely they possess not only the property of consciousness but also religion. Similarly to our very early ancestors and cousins, who tens of thousands of years ago manifested religious traits by burying the dead in common grounds based of kinship of tribal affinity, other mammals demonstrate the underlying quality and complexity to relate to their own based on more than scent, hormones and other biological impositions.

Another example on a different documentary, is that of a female leopard finding a vulnerable baby-monkey in a tree, apparently abandoned by his dead mother, only for her to climb the tree and, instead of killing and eating the delicious prey, started to lick it and surrounding it with its arms in a cautious, maternal grip. The baby-monkey was dead within hours, but not due to lack of efforts from the predator that behaved in total disregard for her stomach, instead opting to try to shelter and protect the foreign offspring. Something overrode her instincts, not only preventing her from killing but also from eating what would normally be an easy meal, even after the small baby-monkey was lying dead in the tree branch.

If animals possess solely instinct and reason (at a much more limited level than we do since they lack rationality), this behavior is beyond illogical in the two cases presented above, and certainly many others not mentioned here. In deep demarcation, it is possible to find human beings that exhibit utter lack of empathy towards life other than their own, not just in respect to animals but also humans. These people we label *psychopaths*, as they show little skill in connecting in an emotional, could be said spiritual, manner with the ones they coexist with. Animals may be dominated by *instinct*, and also possess *reason* in the sense of being able to distinguish a rabbit from a rock, but psychopaths, like all other humans, possess both of the previous plus rationality, i.e. what can be outlined as the inborn ability to create abstract conceptualizations that augment self-awareness and enable purely intellectual apprehension – the ability to think without being limited to direct experience.

A psychopath can be classified as a spiritual Quasimodo, in that it possesses an animal instinct, rationality and reason but little consciousness. These defective human souls are either deformed or diminutive, precluding them from being fully functioning beings when inserted into human societal models that always depended on cooperation and mutual agreement, not to mention respect. Such conclusion also aligns with the fact that most individuals in our species that suffer such spiritual impairment tend to be male, as these are the members of our species who have a lesser bond with the spiritual as they invested more in rationality and instinct. Females on the other hand, have a stronger bond with emotion and empathy, thus being better equipped in what spiritual matters are concerned, although often misusing such advantage due to lack of a sophisticated rational skill set. In the end, men are better at mapping information rationally but their weaker focus on spiritual behavior can more often produce faulty members of the human race that are male, whereas women are left with less ability to interact with the world in a manner as effective as their male counterparts, but are much less likely to be born psychopathic.

As a conclusion, it's far more logical to synthesize morality as an objective law of a metaphysical dimension than the fabricated product of human imagination. Some animals seem to expose such spiritual acuity, while some humans are unable to do so, refuting the idea it's a subjective attribute exclusive to our species alone.

MORAL CONDITIONING

Dios lo ve todo

There is a thought experiment in the field of psychology as well as ethics that is referred to as *the trolley problem*. The idea is as follows: there is a fork in a railway track with ten people tied to it on one side and just one on the other. Given the choice would the test subject switch tracks in order to allow for solely one victim instead of many? There is no time to save all of the people and a choice must be made without any additional alternatives. This issue only poses a serious dilemma for atheists because the decision needs to be made based on quantity alone, something that is not compatible with most religious views. In reality the decision making would be deficient, judging only by the number of people that would die rather by *whom* they are, and consequently what value may be ascribed to them. The truth of the matter is this process involves an activity that is highly favored by atheists – to play God. This explains the impossibility to ensure correct results since humans are not able to perceive qualitative characteristics from afar. Attempts to do so lead to tribalistic patterns of behavior like the ones that can be witnessed in modern Western societies through the lens of Neo-Marxist groups, such as feminists, the woke left, etc. where everyone is packed into groups based on superficial, and therefore easy to recognize traits. The same can be applied to utilitarian views and other atheistic ethical philosophies, as they are deprived of a true and objective sense of meaning or value of the individual.

If another experiment is to be conducted, but this time removing the element of quantity, things will start making slightly more sense. Supposing a woman finds herself on a lifeboat alone and, as the large passenger ship she jumped off sinks, she can see both a young girl in the water in her early teens crying for help, as well as a fat, scruffy-looking, white-bearded older man in his late forties doing the same. They are both equidistant to the lifeboat and it's only possible to save one them due to the large whirlpool caused by the sinking ship growing by the minute, which will soon engulf everyone in sight. The vast majority of people would use the standard human common sense and save the girl: she has more years to live; she poses less of a risk in terms of her helper's safety; she will not be questioning her rescuer's authority. But what if, in a flash of clairvoyance, the woman on the lifeboat sees that the girl would actually turnout to be a whimsical, undisciplined narcissist and eventually, as soon as her rescuer fell asleep, the teen would consume all the available provisions, leading both to die within a couple of days from dehydration. But the woman on the lifeboat was also able to see that, in extreme contrast, rescuing the middle-aged man would lead to their survival and full rescue days later, as he would turn out to be a sailor and could use his expertise to easily deal with a situation he would be acquainted with. Needless to say, given the extra information everyone without exception would choose the older man in detriment of the teenage girl.

Societal context		Action to be permitted/forbidden (by force)	Isolated context	
15 year old girl	30 year old man		15 year old girl	30 year old man
X	X	Rape	X	✓
X	X	Murder	X	✓
X	X	Cannibalism	X	✓

Figure 13: Atheistic vs religious morality

Another factor that needs to be brought into view when engaging in the effort of making moral judgments without God is the predicament morality only exists within a specific context, such as a society, but it changes altogether when leaving it. Say, both a thirty year old man and a fifteen year old teenage girl find themselves stranded on an island, with no possibility of rescue by the outside world (**Figure 13**). The man, being stronger and finding the girl extremely attractive, could resort to raping her repeatedly until satisfied, only to sooner or later choosing to murdering and cannibalizing her in order to keep his hopes of being found alive for a few more days. This would offer him a greater chance of outliving the whole ordeal while a castaway on the island but without denouncing his actions to the world once rescued.

The atheist cannot say what the man did is *wrong*. In fact atheism would impose the natural conclusion that not only he *could* rape, kill and devour the girl, but he *should* do so – they were both going to die irrespective of what he does, so why shouldn't he? The contextual element of repercussions the man may have suffered for his deeds, and the damage it could bring to the girl are gone, because they are no longer entangled in the social environment, and as such the moral directives and ethical prescriptions cannot be put into effect. Whether the atheist agrees or disagrees with such behavior out of *opinion* or *preference,* it needs to be accepted that atheism validates rape, murder and cannibalism. Under atheism, morality depends on the consequence to validate a particular action, whereas religion has the Judgment Day. With the latter, no matter where the rape, murder or cannibalism are to take place, in an isolated island on in the middle of a crowded urban environment, that sentence will inescapably come to pass.

The human condition bounds us not only to poor qualitative judgments, or the complete deferral of such while resorting to a quantitative judgment, but also the forced insertion of moral values within a specific context, without which those values breakdown and become cumbersome or impractical, or both. The conclusion is that we are *conditioned* to acquire moral values in an absolute form from an objective source, i.e. an object independent of our opinions and predilections, or even our own existence. That object, that universe or realm has to be acknowledged as something that exists with its own laws. We exist within it and are a part of it, thus being able to perceive the laws of *Good* and *Evil*, as opposed to imagining or defining them subjectively.

Humbly bowing to an almighty supreme being that observes everything, whom is able to judge without being constricted by limited information or a distorted perspective, delegates the burden of us humans carrying such crushing responsibility. It also enables us to acquire knowledge and wisdom to better handle ourselves under His advice – after all, God *can* stop the rapist-murderer, but if He doesn't (maybe out of love for our freewill since if He interfered now then when would He not do so?) we can only infer He knows better than we do. Without a higher authority, any moral systems devised are conditional of limited perspectives or particular social contexts, all of which are manufactured and organized by a species of frail apes with limited understanding and low degree of intelligence.

TRUE INTUITIVISM

listening to the living, not the dead

Justifying a decision or an action taken with the claims of it being *intuitive* is easy to do and understand, but less so to describe what the *source* of that intuition is. Does it relate to animal instinct? To the subconscious? Past experiences? Mood and hapchance? Or could it be an ethereal source that provided us with such proclivity to do one thing but not the other? Human psychology is certainly too complex to reduce it to an easy answer or explanation, but one could at minimum question the validity of using this component of human psychology altogether, at least when attempting to make informed, rational choices. If one is to use this dark recess within the mind, how sure is he to make a sound decision? *Intuitivism* is the branch of *cognitivism* that makes the claim this is possible, even though it fails to justify *what* the source of the intuition is. In the opposite branch, *naturalism* extracts ethical norms from natural laws and forces, attaching to itself a false pretense of objectivity. If one is to perceive intuition as somewhat related or intertwined with our animal instinct, then it falls into the naturalistic category, because that is what that branch of cognitivism is exactly asserting, or trying to do so. If in contrast intuition relies on the subjectivity of thought, opinion and preference, it would in actuality relegate intuitivism to the opposite branch of metaethics known as *non-cognitivism*, rendering it useless as a form of objective moral decision-making.

The only way to fix the problem is to keep this so called intuition, or intuitive sense, related to something objective, such as a metaphysical source with an ethereal set of laws we can perceive. This would of course demand a set of sensory inputs that would operate in such realm – a place religious people often refer to as the *spiritual world*. Calling it *intuitivism* solely to mask the need for this external factor is disingenuous to say the least, but that is exactly where it appears the word comes from – apparently humans are just able to read situations, as if by magic, while not connected to anything, just pure vacuum. If morality is not to be downgraded to something as lowly as subjective ethical norms – that is to say non-cognitive – *spiritualism* is the only means to turn it into something objective, also answering the question why it can be only found within one's self. Unfortunately that word has too been butchered by the seekers of conversations with the dead and other types of con-artists, with the only option left being to reinterpret the meaning of intuitivism.

We humans are all dwellers of the spiritual world but, just like in the material world, we process and interpret any information received by us in a personal, somewhat different manner, within the boundaries of a shared judicial framework. Just like some bodies have better vision, others better hearing, so will some souls have better engagement with love, altruism, compassion, integrity, etc. "We are not all born the same" – statement that does not represent solely our material selves but also our immaterial presence. Occam's razor would be satisfied with this conclusion, as opposed to retrofitting awkward, dissonant and inconsistent explanations, only to fulfill the thirst of the ones who, unilaterally, chose not to believe.

CHAPTER 4

The End of Science

A LAND OF CONTRAST

where we are

Between light and dark, order and chaos, life and death, perfection and imperfection, good and evil, positive and negative: existence is an ocean of duality between these and many more abstract dichotomies. Without opposite, contradictory qualities, reason would not be able to operate. The universe is only but a small portion of this land that encompasses everything that exists, without exception. To conceptualize existence beyond space and time, cause and effect, it's indispensable to infer everything ethereal, intangible and imaginary depends entirely on this divide. But what is there between the two?

If God is to be unique, infinite and unbegotten, it requires exclusive characteristics not attributed to anything else, but that permeate all there is, until there is nothing at all. God is the origin of everything, thence the epicenter of an imaginary circle up until that circle fades completely away into oblivion – that is to say complete non-existence.

Referring to **Figure 14**, the end result is a land of contrast between two things and two things alone: God and the Absence of God. The light, but also the darkness, engulf the entirety of the circle that henceforth shall be referred to as the *Existential Continuum*, that is a multitude of layers that make up everything that exists, from the material universe to the spiritual, and possibly an infinite number of other realms and dimensions. The closer these existential planes are to God, the more they are graced with His attributes and, conversely, the further away, the less His presence can be witnessed. In the physical universe, the laws that rule it are evidence of His presence, but are in no way comparable to the laws of the spiritual universe that lies a *layer* above to it.

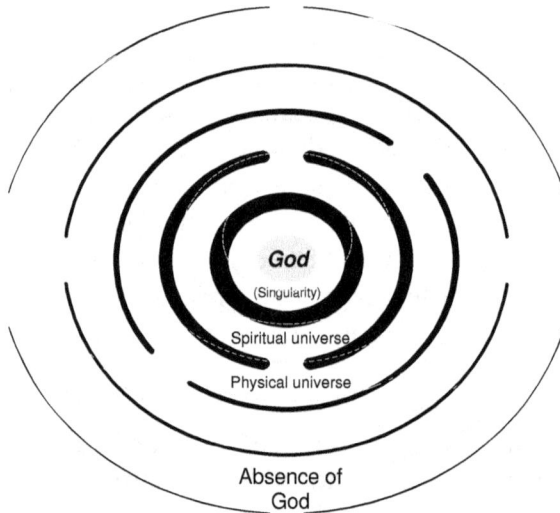

Figure 14: The Existential Continuum

The more distanced one of these layers is from God, the more it delves into non-existence, and thus the less contrast there is until eventually complete darkness, the *Yin,* will be all that is left. In the opposite direction, inwards into the *Singularity,* more and more light will abound, the *Yang,* until God is reached – the divine, infinite, indivisible source of existence, love, life and anything else possibly and imaginably conceptualized as positive.

THE DUAL NATURE OF BEING

what we are

Humans are therefore a product of both the material world and the spiritual one. If death for atheists is merely the end of biological function, for those who do not suffer from such rational myopia and spiritual cataracts, there is more to existence than meets the eye – both literally and figuratively. There's plenty of evidence that this reductivist approach fails miserably when trying to explain things such as morality, freewill, existential dread, meaning of life, love, compassion, altruism, etc. Just like an iceberg has its biggest portion under water, humans are mostly inserted into the material world. We have been animal lifeforms for millions of years, turning us into experts of this realm, featuring multiple senses, instincts and biological traits. But the tip of the iceberg (seen on **Figure 15**), the part that is always visible above the water, can be seen very much like our soul, the spiritual part in all of us. If our animal nature is dominant, it may frequently obfuscate our spiritual inputs, leading a lot of people to devote themselves to their most mediocre, and also ephemeral part. But unlike with this metaphor, the part that is submerged cannot see anything through the surface of water, rendering it completely blind to any information lying therein. Only the smaller part of the iceberg, its tip, is able to cognize anything that is present and comes to pass above the surface, i.e. the immaterial world.

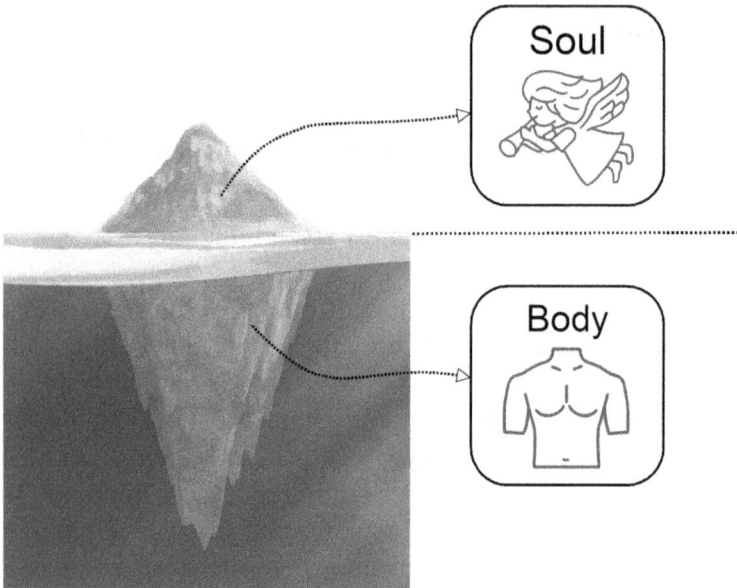

Figure 15: The two existential realms

Just like in the cartoons, there is indeed a little angel next to our ear speaking to us on every decision we make, or at the very least the more significant ones. It can be called our conscience, Holy Ghost, Shakra, intuition or many other things but it's inherently the inner voice that delivers guidance beyond the animal instinct. But unlike with the cartoons, next to the other ear there isn't a little devil, but instead a tall and big demon the size of our body – because that is exactly what it is. Our physical, animal ego and instincts prevail most of the time and dominate us, unless domesticated. To move away from such menial existence, avoiding a rudimentary life experience dependent on our animal selves, care must be taken to not sever the umbilical cord to the timid voice coming from the tip of the iceberg, since it's easy to be under complete subservience of greed, gluttony, lust, wrath, envy, pride, sloth or any other hedonistic and egotistic, deadly addictions that will relentless and routinely attempt to bribe us.

THE ARGUMENT FROM EVIL

the blind see no darkness

An age-old atheistic provocation, in defiance of the existence of an almighty creator, is "If God exists, why does He allow cancer to be?" An omnipotent, omniscient God would not allow such erratic imperfection to afflict the innocent, most will presume. Even though religious people often struggle to answer such question, there are severe flaws with this weak attempt at taunting believers and make them put their faith into question. Some reflection and scrutiny can lead to finding an initial contradiction: if God were to abide by human will, would that entity be worthy of such title? Delving a bit deeper it's possible to ascertain that were humans to run a referendum to vote on whether God should indeed banish cancer for eternity, what if a future generation changes opinion, forcing God to change the rules again? Even worse, what if an existing alien civilization disagrees with such vote and, upon meeting them and assuming compatible inter-species procreation were to take place, what rules would be applied to the newborn? The main issue with this argument, like with most narratives that are designed to put God into question, is that atheists replace God trying to make themselves the arbiters of truth and the supervisors of the laws of existence. Religious people can humbly claim God's designs to be beyond their knowledge or understanding, which is a perfectly legitimate statement – letting God be God – whereas the atheist needs to play that role himself, due to lack of better choice, thereby failing miserably.

But looking even deeper into the issue, there is a final nail in the atheist coffin, a solution that this book brings forth, with high hopes of it presenting a true endgame. If God were to preemptively interfere with the universe and prevent cancer, why stop there? Once he distorted his own design and changed the rules of the game, why not rid living organisms of any disease? Wouldn't that paradoxically eliminate all bacteria and viruses that were indelibly important, even essential, for life to form? Going further, shouldn't God prevent the evil doer from relishing in the act of inflicting pain onto others, out of possessing a devious will? What about preventing carnivores from existing, as they eat other animals, causing them pain and their inevitable demise? Indeed, a *just* God would eliminate any animal life, as herbivores require to feed off plants, which are living organisms as well. But the slippery slope doesn't end there, as God would not refer to human opinion to what to eliminate, with the universe being stripped of any chaos, as He would forbid an asteroid from hitting Earth, or black holes from swallowing stars. The end result would turn out there would be no universe at all. And inferring God would exercise the same logic and apply His will to eradicate anything imperfect, there would be nothing at all. No universes or dimensions, no material or immaterial entities, nothing except for God Himself.

With this, we reach the end-of-life of the argument that states "if God existed, certainly *Evil* would not be allowed to be", as that is the only way life *can* exist *outside* God, but still bathed by His grace, His presence – what in Eastern philosophy is usually called the *Yang*. Nothing can exist without God, as He is synonymous with Life, Good, Beauty, Order, Perfection, Light, Harmony, Love, Infinity, Truth and indeed, Existence itself. For all other things to exist, they cannot be *within* God, as they would be one with Him – an indivisibly divine singularity. But His presence permeates everything that *is*, with the exclusion of absolute Nothingness. Anything in-between these to forces, God and the Absence of God, is bathed by the Almighty, Omniscient, Omnipotent, Omnipresent *élan vital* we call God.

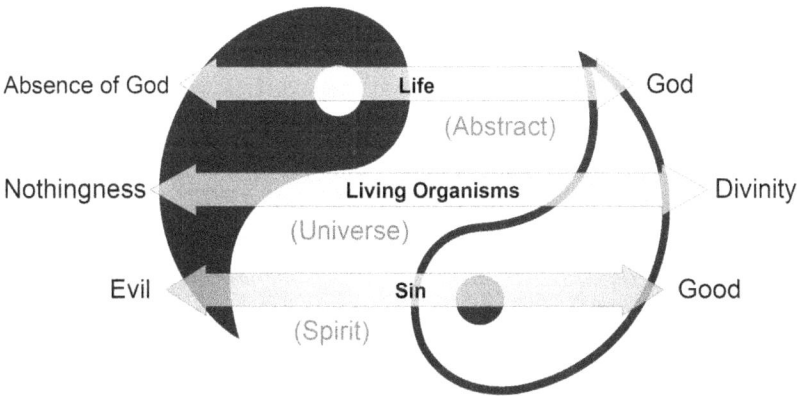

Figure 16: The driving force behind existence

In a straightforward analogy, a blind man does not know what the color *black* is, as, being born that way, he has not mastered *white* or any other colors for that effect, i.e. he doesn't have a metric that he can use to compare *black* to. The same way, were we to be born in heaven, *Good* would not be perceivable since *Evil* had not been experienced in the slightest. We are faulty, imperfect creatures and that is what in effect completes us as unique, indivisible individuals, leaving the experience of evil as a precondition of the universe we are born in. Without that contrast nothing can be outside the single, indivisible entity that God is.

As per **Figure 16**, All the *stuff* – the ingredients in the soup of existence – that makes up the Existential Continuum can be classified as Yin and Yang, which would not exist without the amalgam of God and the Absence of God, Divinity and Nothingness, Good and Evil. Life can only exists outside God due to the state of non-existence that is the Absence of God. Good cannot exist without Evil, as there would be nothing to define it as, or compare it to. The composition of these contrasting factors and forces are what make up this multi-dimensional reality, as there is no order without chaos, neither there is a hint of chaos without order.

MULTI-DIMENSIONAL BEINGS

walking on all four

According to atheistic belief, humans are solely molecular structures, just like any other animal, plant or rock. Each individual body, inanimate or otherwise, has no more *value* to the universe than the other. Under the scientific discipline of physics whichever formulas, equations or laws are applied, all life in the universe is made of biological organisms constructed through an evolutionary process that resulted in less or more complex machines – but still machines nevertheless. All were forged from the same soup of star dust blasted across the universe, only for them to be subsequently molded by the laws of gravity, thermodynamics and all other collaborators. However, a lot of questions remain unanswered that keep humans (atheists included) from fully accepting the reformist ideas of being just machines devoid of a purpose or any meaning, roaming aimlessly within this vast structure made of space and time.

The universe is traditionally defined as being four dimensional: one dimension for time and three for space. However, this manner of interpreting the information our sensory inputs supply us with is erroneous, as spacial dimensions should be classified as sub-dimensions of space itself, with the latter being level with time, thus making the universe a two-dimensional affair. So a new perspective should be introduced to configure the universe as two-dimensional, at the very least at the physical level. But if in what particles and energy is concerned two dimensions are enough, the same cannot be said for aspects of our cognition that transcend the laws of physics, of time and space. Consciousness is the act of self-awareness, plus the necessity to relate and co-exist with other beings, who can be inferred to feature the same level of of incorporeal cognition. It's not the same to pet a cat or a dog, or a snake or a spider. Even if all these creatures just mentioned in practice can be domesticated, the degree of interaction is hardly the same, not only out of lack of intellectual sophistication but also consciousness. **Figure 17** can aid in the understanding of this idea.

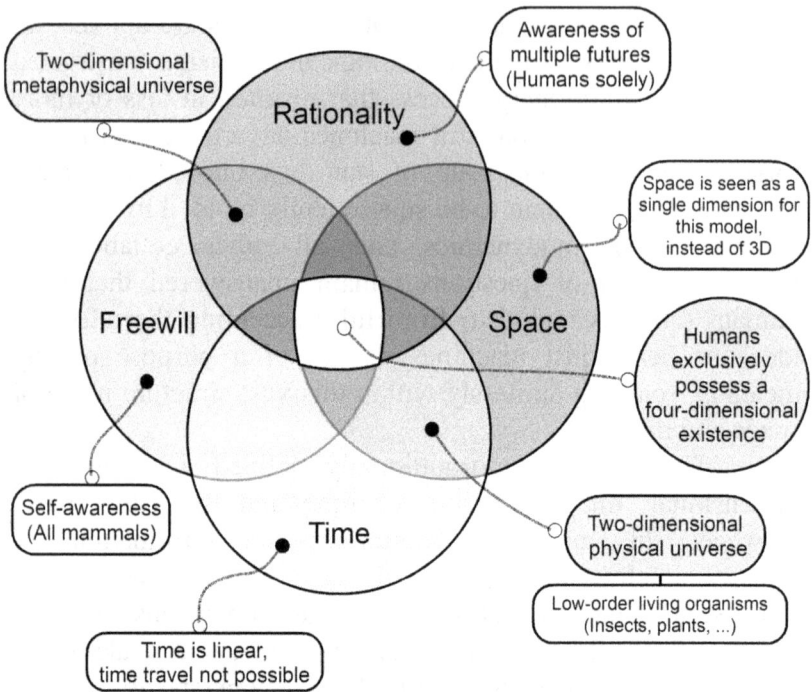

Figure 17: The four dimensions that make up the universe

All mammals can be speculated to be conscious beings, but the same cannot be read from the mechanical behavior of the vast majority of the other classes of animals, if not their totality. This would constitute mammals as being three-dimensional creatures, made of space, time and consciousness. But one of the mammals stands out as unique – the one that is not only conscious but also rational. If *reason* can be outlined as the ability to distinguish truth from falsehood, such that all animals possess it, like the ability for a lion to have a drink from a pool water but not from a pool of oil, *rationality* can be distinguished as something altogether unique, as unlike with reason, rationality allows for abstract thought. Amongst many things, such as mathematics, geometric shapes, tools and technologies, human beings can also plan things ahead of time in a notional manner, i.e. we are able to see the consequences of our actions and methodologies in advance.

Without delving too deep into M-theory speculation (because it's not a subject of this book, but a future one) and the ten dimensions of existence – which would be crunched down to eight dimensions, if interpreting space as it should be, a single dimension – the third dimension (fifth in the presently used model) could be read as *consciousness*, i.e. the ability to make choices based on a higher state of mind. This means the rabbit, the lion and the dog are *aware* of the choice they make, that is they are aware of a future in front of them, thence this can be construed as being creatures of space-time-spirit. But the only animal that is able to be fully aware of the multitude of choices in front of it is the species of ape called homo-sapiens. It has the uncanny ability to engage in abstract experience (noesis at its finest), giving this species the quality of speculating about metaphysical conundrums such as the awareness of multiple futures, existential dread and questioning the purpose of its own existence. The resulting conclusion is that the third dimension of *consciousness* permits the creatures who dwell in it to possess freewill – the act of choosing with one own's agency, which under the M-theory would be described as *possible worlds*, translating to the act of being able to choose. Whereas the dimension of *rationality* gifts its dwellers the abstract knowledge of *being aware* of possessing that very same freewill, this time to allow multiple choices out of many, described under the M-theory as *all possible worlds*.

Intelligent design, based on a different approach that would not resort to a petty god whimsically manipulating the universe as he sees fit, could be used to justify consciousnesses as a determining factor in the macro evolution of mammals – the most complex lifeforms we are aware of, and therefore the most superior ones in terms of *existential value*. Conscious animals are able to evolve to a much greater degree of complexity due to this extra dimension they are part of, as it will influence their growth as a species, including allowing them to evolve into a new classifiable sub-species or entirely new species. This brings forth a logical explanation for the many problems molecular biologists have found when trying to warrant the extreme complexity of the genetic variation between animals – especially the most complex ones – and the very short time span available for such evolution to take place, which is close to a meager 4.5 billion years since the Earth was born, a lot of which is likely to have been lifeless altogether.

THE ARGUMENT FROM FREE WILL

the destiny is now

Does the existence of an omniscient God contradict freewill? If He sees everything, isn't fate predetermined, and therefore our *will* is nothing more than an illusion? In the ancient Greek tale of Oedipus Rex, his father, the king, was given a prophecy that stated his firstborn (Oedipus), once grown, would murder him and then marry his wife, the queen. Out of fear, the king ordered his own baby-son killed but hearing this the queen had her servant sent away, taking with her the baby to a very distant kingdom. Later in life Oedipus, unaware of his lineage, returns to his birthplace, unknowingly fulfilling the prophecy by killing his father and marrying his mother. The (im)moral of the story is, no matter how many turns life takes, no matter how many contrivances we concoct, destiny is greater than human *will*, presenting itself as an unavoidable aid in fate always catching up.

For atheists like neuroscientist Sam Harris, freewill can be fully reduced the reactions of the brain to its sensory stimuli, with the neuro-scientific field studying synapses in the effort to explain such interactions. To these atheists there is nothing more than the activity within the brain, as opposed to the mind as an ethereal object. This would, of course, render freewill not free at all – in fact that is the assertion that Harris makes, even though he defers the *self*, and all its existential qualms and wills, to the typical atheistic plateau of obscure value. That is, even if you are not free, it's still *you* (whatever that can be delineated as under the atheistic prism), and therefore your actions and the 'will' they derive from can be constituted as agency. In less words, even though you are a machine, you are still made responsible for any effect caused by the machine's interaction with the world. What leads to this conclusion is impossible to tell, since it's formed by another machine who's input, in all its considerations and being named Harris or anything else, is just as valid as any other machine's – at least of the automaton brand *Homo-sapiens*.

Engaging in the exercise of pushing freewill away from the realm of *nature* and into the realm of *nurture* is not necessary in the slightest – quite the contrary. When transferring freedom of will to the domain of subjectivity, cracks begin to appear, until the whole argument collapses, as do all the disputes that belong to the domain of atheism. Freedom of choice requires agency, which in turn requires absolute independence of any governing laws, which would otherwise shape that *will* externally, making it not free but a servant of cause and effect. To escape this cage, the mind needs to be its own *noumenon*, i.e. an object who's existence is independent of any other objects, while being dependent on a body that is characterized as a *phenomenon*, since it exists as a portion of the universe. The end result is what can be analytically called a *noumenon-phenomenon*.

One could step into a metaphorical beach where an immense sheet of sand, as smooth as flat as it can possibly be, lies still. There are no ocean waves harassing its surface, nor winds perturbing its calm. Then, out of nowhere, a small footprint appears. It's faint and almost indistinguishable from the rest of the sand at first, but soon a clear imprint starts taking form and gaining shape. Ridges start to materialize, indenting this unique, singular imprint into the immense sheet of sand. Behold, this is not a footprint in the slightest, but a *mindprint*. As the noumenon-phenomenon lives, it experiences, acts, chooses, causing the imprint in the sand to constantly change, until it takes its final shape due to the phenomenon part collapsing as it runs out of time, with both detaching themselves from the prior arrangement leaving only the noumenon left. This mind-body (noumenon-phenomenon) duality leads to the shaping of the mindprint that, albeit being wrought by experience, possesses agency within itself due to its noumenal nature, allowing it to freely make choices in a self-growing ritual. The purpose of this exercise is to establish the necessity of the noumenal nature of the mind, instead of crunching both the mind and the body into the realm of the phenomenal that is the physical universe.

Freed of the dictatorship of the laws of physics, being promoted to a noumenon, the mind can independently make choices, take actions and command the body, the latter still constrained by the laws of the material world. This results in a fully qualified *agent* that is thus accountable and made responsible for any consequences he may be the cause of.

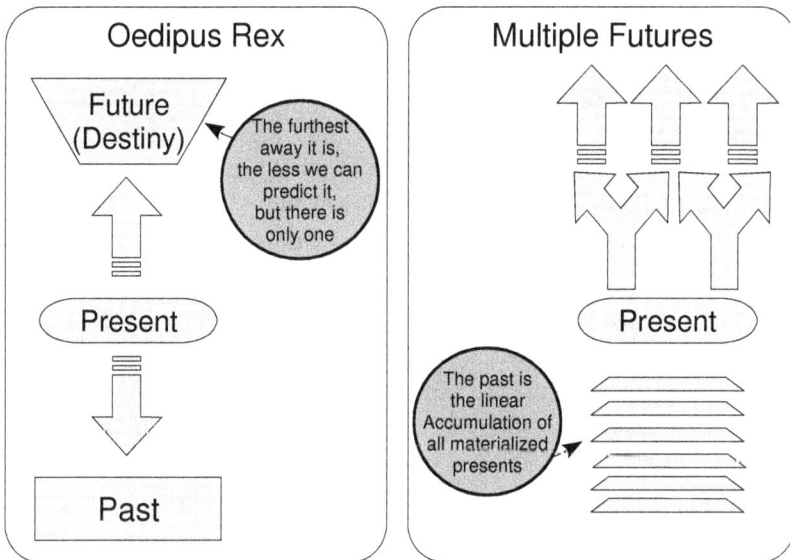

Figure 18: Fate versus multiple-futures

This freedom, however, only exists in the present, as we cannot act in the future, nor change the past. Because we are rational beings, we can see the multiple choices ahead of us, resulting in us being able to encapsulate in our minds, in a fully abstract manner, the predictability of our actions, even if not in absolute terms, at least partially. The M-theory should be changed to deal with multiple-futures instead of multiple-worlds. There are no multiple worlds or universes, certainly not ones we humans are attached too, but many futures that lie ahead of us (**Figure 18**). As such, the present cannot be foreseen since it's happening now. It's where our bodies exist, our brains think, and our actions take place.

In conclusion, freewill only exists in the present, and since God cannot predict the present as that constitutes paradox, He can only foreknow the many futures ahead of us – even if these are to be counted in the trillions, were He to look at the whole of mankind put together. This logical averment resolves to no contradiction between an omniscient God and the idea of humans having full agency when taking actions or making choices. Without fate, without being preconditioned to a set destiny, we are fully free in the present, with the future representing the almost endless possibilities ahead of us, within the constrictions of time and space. We should stop dwelling in the past, to instead create our paths by existing in the present, dependent only on what futures are available to us. We can't instantly teleport to Mars and set base there, but we sure can work hard and discover, innovate, understand, grow, and inevitably Mars will be ours. Understand the past, work with the present, build the future. That is the purpose of our existence and a way to interpret the meaning of human life within our own perspective and limited understanding.

THE TREE OF KNOWLEDGE

embracing the truth

Until the 15th century, when Polish astronomer Nicolaus Copernicus (1473 – 1543 A.D.) developed an heliocentric model of the universe with the Sun, rather than the Earth, at the epicenter and as the main factor to determine planetary movement, the commonly accepted model was known as geocentrism. This model placed the Earth at the center of all there is out of religions reasons: (Genesis 1:27) "God created man in His own image" states he was to take center stage, with the remaining of the universe serving mere decorative purposes. The Copernican model only started being widely accepted a century later, give or take, with its main champion, Galileo Galilei (1564 – 1642 A.D.) nearly paying with his life to defend it. Among many of the problems that the geocentric model contained, one of the most particular ones were the planetary orbits, since if the Sun is not at the center of what was referred for thousands of years as the universe (in modern day terms, the Solar System), then these orbits could not simply be circular relative to planet Earth, since through observation of the other planets, such as Mars, these would not be in the correct position all times. To fix this issue, the Hellenic Greek philosopher and astronomer Claudius Ptolcmy (circa 100 – 170 A.D.) had suggested the orbits of all other planets to be incorporated into *epicycles* (**Figure 19**). This way not only the planet would orbit the Earth but its motion would also enter retrogressive cycles that would permit to explain the motion of all five planets known at the time, with the favorable added bonus of justifying the presence of our planet at the center of the cosmos.

It can thus be seen how adaptive humans can be to a belief or preference, regardless of the information provided to them. The contemporaneous term for this is *confirmation bias*. In the atheist's cookbook, there is a similar system to geocentrism that could be named the e*gocentric* model of the universe, where extreme resistance is made to anything the individual cannot experience materially. If it does not conform to the perspective of the atheist, nor does it fit within the premises stipulated by him, it's summarily thrown out. This places scientific knowledge at the pedestal of the truth, that is, what we can understand and verify via the empirical sciences is accepted, but anything else is subjected to skepticism. What cannot be posited by studying natural phenomena cannot be verified, thence it's thrown into the *unfalsifiable* bucket. Human knowledge surrenders to *positivism*, depending exclusively on the study of the material world while severing the umbilical cord with the spiritual world.

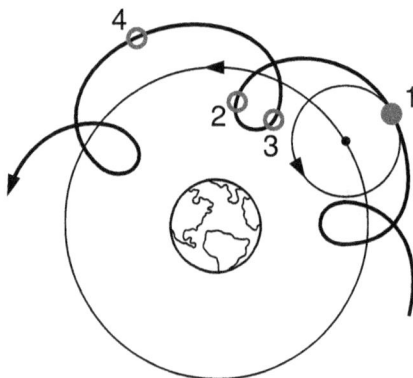

Figure 19: Ptolemy's epicycles

Regrettably to the atheist crowd, science cannot disprove spiritual matters because they are transcendental to physics. Constraining all knowledge, and epistemology itself, to the demands of empirical data is nothing short of a failed strategy, as it depends on the prerogative that all that is true arises from such source. But in fact this is what atheists do, as they have circumscribed their views to the belief that every ounce of human knowledge is subordinate to the natural world – the realm of space and time, or simply put the universe. But using

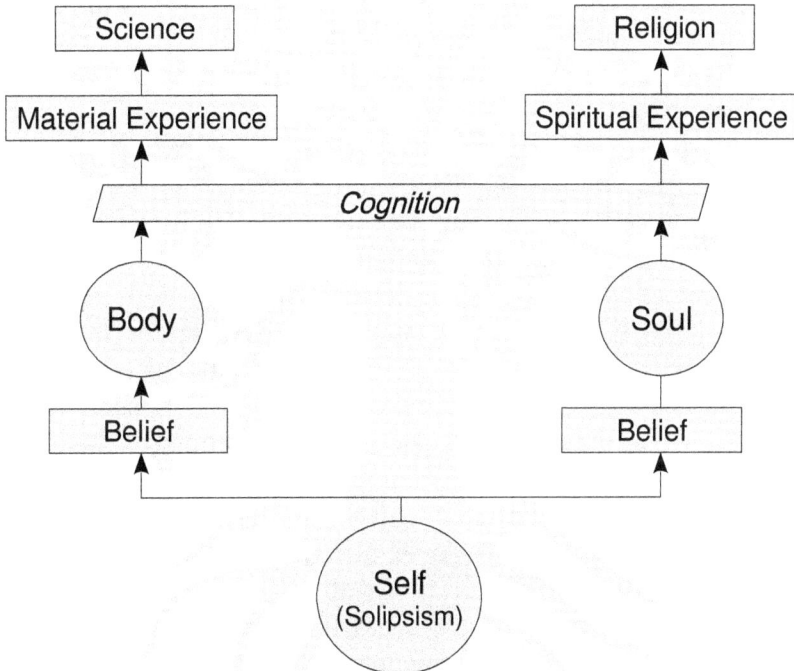

Figure 20: The Tree of Knowledge

rational thought, removed from all bias of any type of belief, will lead to the *Tree of Knowledge* (**Figure 20**) for a description on *how* human experience actually functions.

Before all, there is the *self*, the sentient, self-aware being that thinks therefore he is. Not accepting the *subject* as the starting point of all knowledge is absurd and would also infer that 'non-acceptance' from originating from another *subject* that requires that very sentience to form their opinion in first place so it could be considered. Thus the subject is the *self*, the noumenon, the essence of the being that can experience, and without which there is no noesis or *nous* – the intellect, the immaterial mind, the activity while *being*. The noumenon cannot function unless linked to a phenomenon within another noumenon – the human being needs a conductor to bring information regarding another object he exists within, otherwise he would experience nothing. Thus, the body exists as a phenomenon within the noumenon we call the universe, channeling all information, acquired from its sensory inputs while engaging in physical experience, through the brain, the central processing unit, into the immaterial mind – the self. This process is known as *cognition* and allows us to use science as a tool to understand the realm of natural phenomena, also known as the universe made of space and time.

However, all scientific knowledge is fully dependent on belief, otherwise one could question the validity of the universe, and even go as far as question the existence of the self as an illusion. If all physical cognitive experience is delimited by belief, why disregard the *other* belief – the one necessary to explain subject matter that the cosmos and its laws don't understand, such as existential qualms, morality, love and the like? The soul can then be taken as a spiritual body, a phenomenon within the spiritual realm, with its sensory inputs providing the mind with the end results of metaphysical cognition. To differentiate from each belief as if one can be validated more than the other is not only preposterous but also intellectually dishonest, which is exactly what atheists do recurrently in an attempt to demystify science and mythologise religion.

The Bible assures us of this conclusion saying: (John 20:29) "[...] Blessed are they who did not *see,* and yet believed", or to put it in a simplified form, each body to each realm. Humans are the end product of the combined cognitive experience both our bodies provide us with, and deferring one body to the domain of 'nonsensical' is itself, nonsensical. Thus, anything we *know* is wholly derived from belief, without which one must resort to hypocrisy to presume the objectivity of the physical reality, but not the metaphysical one.

THE REGULATORY IDEAL

bound to see

Human knowledge isn't limitless, and will never be. For millennia philosophers pondered about the nature of the objects within themselves and the way we observe these objects in order to synthesize them into our human minds. A shape, a color, a scent or whichever sense we resort to, it only provides us with a human-dependent interpretation, that is a translation from what the object really is into the way humans can understand it. This process may be fully species-conditioned, as we are yet to encounter another species we could debate this concepts with. Another sentient species, extra-terrestrial out of need, can potentially read information obtained from the universe in a widely different manner – even if they carried similar senses to our own, nothing guarantees their mental visualization of reality to be necessarily the same. *Human truths* (as per **Figure 21**) are then truths based on human perspective that we presume to be mentally processed identically by each individual of our species. In reality it's not possible to know if all humans see the color 'red' indistinguishably from all other members of the species – what is a color anyway, and how can one define it outside an illusory phonetic representation? It's non-translatable into anything else, including words, sounds, temperatures, etc. conferring it an innate value to the individual sensing it. Thus, the assumption that all humans see 'red' in a shared fashion is indelible to the human condition. If one were to step outside this boundary that would refer to an act that atheists are irredeemably tied to – playing God.

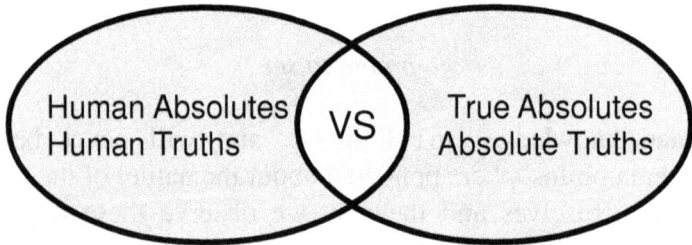

Figure 21: The Truth under a human vs absolute prism

On the other end of the spectrum there are *absolute truths*. These are to be fully grasped by an omniscient entity, as any other type of entity, no matter how powerful or intelligent, would require an interpretative layer to acquire any knowledge, rendering it subjective, and as such 'impure'. Only an almighty being can *see* things as they really are in themselves, in their true form without any sort of translation. The *meaning of life* can be understood from a *human truth* point of view: to experience, to discover, to understand, to grow. It is to live life itself through the enjoyment of trying new things, as opposed to, for example, always playing the same song or reading the same magazine. If spirituality is objective, within one self, it also belongs to the *human truths* category, as anything brought to us by the spiritual senses is also interpretive and limited by human comprehension. Being bound by the human condition, we can accept these truths to constitute the regulatory ideal for humanity. Overstepping the bounds of the human ability to understand only leads to confusion as we are not able to reach beyond what we are capable of, while surrendering to subjectivity accrues to the disarray of human knowledge, epistemology and all our cognitive states.

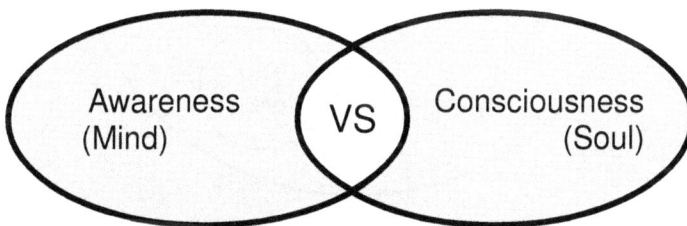

Figure 22: Difference between the mind and the soul

As a part of a whole, all humans are inferred to see everything within the extent of *human truths*, and the more information we acquire about a specific subject matter, the more it enters the category of what is the *Known*. Outside this category, there are the things that are knowable to humans, now or in a close or a distant future, which are referred to as the *Unknown*. Extending into infinity there are all the things that can be known, but are completely outside the human forum or possibility of becoming

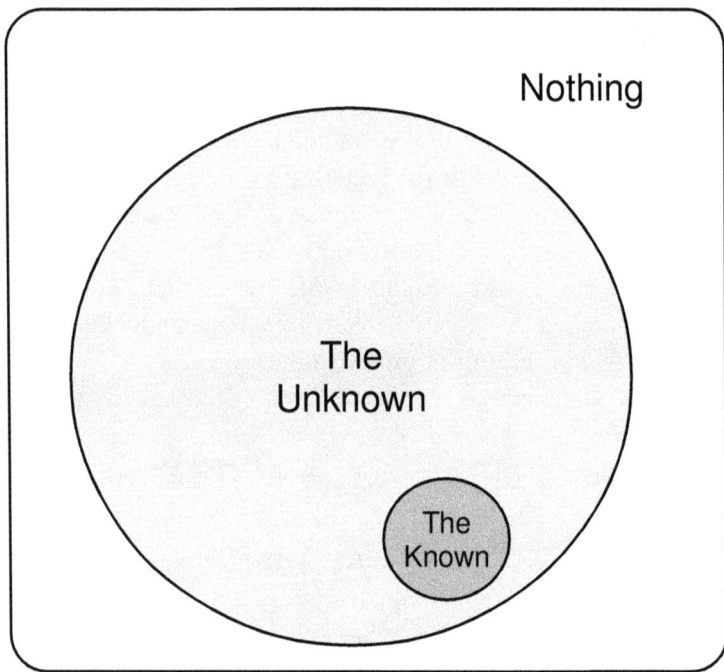

Figure 23: The three scopes of human knowledge

part of human knowledge, and forever will be so (see **Figure 23**). No matter how long our civilization lasts; no matter how much we evolve; no matter what kind of life after death we encounter, certain things are simply unreachable to us. To this, we refer to *Nothing*, what can be classified as the unknown that will never be known. These three categories encapsulate the entirety of the *Existential Continuum*, with absolute nothing, or non-existent things, being placed in the *Nothing* category of any *human* truths alongside what is unknowable to us.

THE MEANING OF LIFE

meant to mean

Deep thinkers will experience existential dread more frequently than others, but everyone may go through an existential depression at least once in their life-time. What are we doing here? What is the purpose of the universe? Why is there something rather than nothing? Is there an underlying *meaning* to it all? The honest atheist engages in *passive denialism*, either by deferring all questions they are too unintelligent to comprehend or by questioning the validity of the doubtfulness itself: why ask any of these questions at all? Just enjoy life and disregard the above as concoctions of the human mind under the misguidance of religion. The faux-atheist takes a different approach, allowing himself to pull answers out of thin air using dogmatic arguments, often stolen from religious doctrine, in what can be called *active denialism*. In the former, they passively disregard the enigma, whereas in the latter they resort to deceit and trickery to pretend to have an answer. But in both cases the atheist is left with a meaningless existence, even if the active denialist manufactures meaning from things such as beauty and well-being, and the passive denialist just downright ignores the meaninglessness of his own existence – that is the brunt they must both carry, as represented in **Figure 24**.

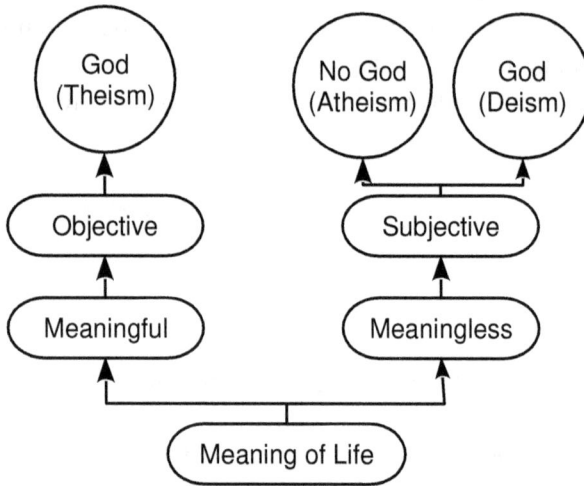

Figure 24: The objectivity or subjectivity of the meaning of life (based on belief)

The religious individual however, carries the sword of knowledge offered by the gods he bows to, and a shield of faith to protect himself from fear and dread. Wherever he goes, there is the acceptance of an higher authority, an almighty overseer of all things. This owner of infinite wisdom is watching from above the flimsy mortal soul that is engulfed in doubt, sorrow and phobia. Knowing there is more than the corporeal reality our body inhabits, and that there is a light at the end of the tunnel, no matter how far it appears to be from us, brings solace and comfort to the believer (**Figure 25**). He may not be fully savvy in the matters of the ethereal, but his inner peace comes from the credence the burden is not for him to bear, but instead the duty is left to the almighty entity he worships in his quotidian existence. To him, this esoteric meaning is tied to an object, rendering it as real as anything in material world. But to the atheist this is nothing but a pointless quest to attach a fabricated value, or meaning, to something he knows cannot carry any significance, no matter how deluded he compels himself to be.

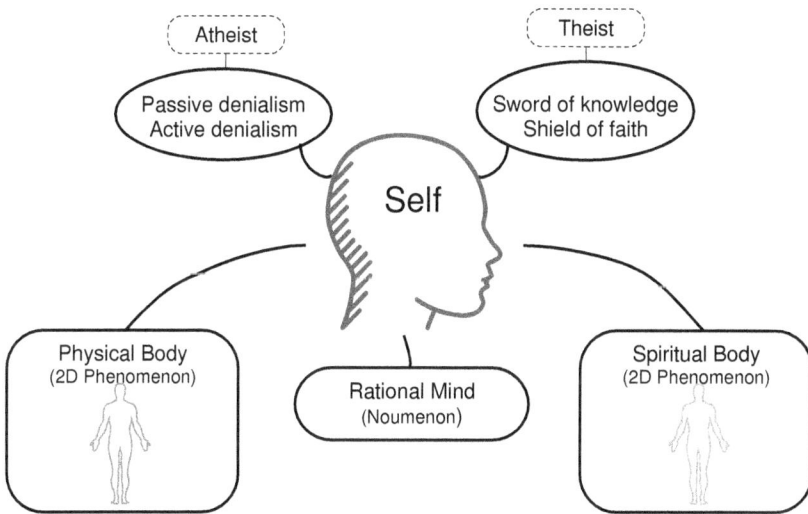

Figure 25: The triplicit nature of the human being and its correlation with existential dread

Besides the need for spiritual faith to find closure in what one's purpose is, a further question arises: how do we *experience* the meaning of life? Why is it there a query and where did it come from? If we are made of space, time, conscience and reason, one of these dimensions has to bring the matter into our minds. Humans can't create things from nothing, such that we can't create new colors in our heads even if we tried to. All we apprehend intellectually comes from an external source, a set of multidimensional noumenons exogenous to our mind. But even if entering the realm of atheistic fantasy, and propose one were to be able to achieve such feat and ideate a brand new color, how is he to convey it to someone else? There is no dimension he shares with others that could be used as a medium to transfer such information. The color would be left alone inside his head, in a ceaselessly solipsistic state, absenting him from any ability to influence and dazzle the minds of his piers with the newly found chromatic wizardry.

One can conclude that this ultimate meaning, the meaning of life, is evidence we experience metaphysics not bound by time and space. If you are solely a portion, or chunk, of the universe, a clump of cells made of star dust, you cannot create things outside its bounds or limitations, as you are constricted by its laws. It requires a third dimension of *consciousness* as a receptor for the feeling of dread of non-existence, and a fourth dimension carrying us to the highest levels of reason, granting us *awareness* of our consciousness in an abstract form (**Figure 22**). If the *meaning of life* cannot be created by the human mind, and cannot be found in this fishbowl we call the space-time universe, then it must forcibly belong to another dimensional factor we are tied to. We must be present in the domain of where both existential dread and the meaning of life can be witnessed, felt, cognized.

Furthermore, the meaning of life is the only *meaning* we truly perceive. Other meanings are euphemisms for cause and effect (or consequence) we observe in nature. These are scientific meanings that ascribe to the only pure, original *meaning*. If a bird sings, there is no actual *meaning* behind it, neither is there a meaning if a droplet of water falls from the sky – these are just manifestations of a universe where one thing leads to another in an endless chain of events without purpose or reason. Unless they are knotted to something else that is. Something much greater than particles, energy and their perpetual, synergistic dance under the laws of the inferior domain we were also born into.

CHAPTER 5

The Selfish God

THE BIRTH OF RELIGION

before and now

When Europeans colonized the four corners of the planet, all peoples they made contact with, from the largest civilization to the smallest human clan, were found to have at least one god as an entry point to the spiritual world. Many had no wheel, others no written languages, but all had religion – and somehow they all also had stories about the moon and the sun. The reason for this parallel is that humans will not invent, create or imagine the same thing in unison. If atheists were genuine, they would have to acknowledge this fact renders the idea of God being made-up extremely unlikely, just the same way that if it was possible for the moon not to be seen from a specific point in the world and that place was populated by a sedentary group of humans, it would be downright impossible for them to have stories about our solitary cosmic satellite. They wouldn't be claiming it's an eye in the sky, the night sun, a god, or whether it's made of cheese or is inhabited by alien creatures. This establishes the religiosity of humanity, and how innate to us it is, because claiming every group of humans around the globe, at a primordial level or another, envisaged such concept is downright preposterous.

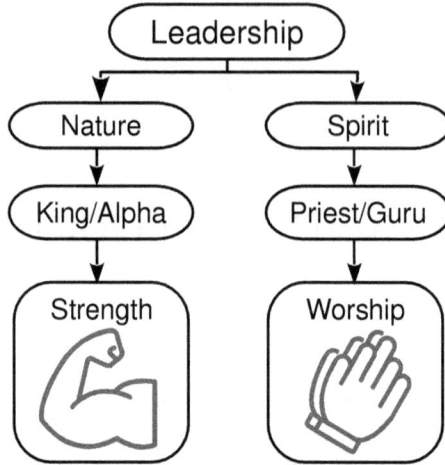

Figure 26: The indelible nature of religion within humanity

Atheists tend to take the preferred route of assuming that morality led humans to become religious, in their typical tactic of utilizing confirmation bias. However one could say both either walked hand-in-hand or religion is actually what defined the contours of morality. When studying the animal kingdom, it is easy to assert that savage beasts that live together are naturally structured around the survival of the fittest – the leader that provides the best conditions to the pack, pride, herd, band, etc. will take charge. Humans still possess this exact characteristic that translates to a king, emperor, president, chieftain, pharaoh, etc. who can be perceived, just like within the wild kingdom, as the alpha leader. This type of position is therefore an extension of what humans used to be a part of, and still are to some magnitude: creatures that evolved within the natural ecosystem often referred to as *Mother Earth*. But something clearly distinguishes us from all animals – something one could dare suggest is a precondition to human evolution and maturity, as per **Figure 26**. Enter the spiritual leader. Designate him the shaman, the priest, the guru, the monk, the clergy, or in a straightforward manner the dignitary of the divine entity. This head of spiritual affairs, the representative of God and all things insubstantial, did not rule through physical strength or ability to wield power, but instead fulfilled the emotional and psychological needs of the tribe, catering for the weak, the sick and the vulnerable.

One could say, without this type of leader there would be no human civilization. We would resort solely to the brute force approach to have strong and competent leaders, not bowing to the ones that, being weak, tended to our spiritual needs. There was indeed a great deal more respect when listening to the ecclesiastic than the forced respect that came from intimidation of the alpha male, while surrounded by his troops. The human mind developed a non-animal sense of hierarchy that helped push us away from being just another creature in the wild. Even if the separation of church and state took its time, humans did get there – at least some of them did.

The fact of the matter is religion is indelible to human civilization and ignorantly devaluing all its contributions towards it is nothing more than philistine hostility. It does not constitute a needless pursuit of imaginary wizards so humans can feel better about themselves, but instead it's the most important driving force pushing us out of the natural jungle environment and all its limitations.

RELIGION CAME FIRST

a boulder on its back

One of the main reasons why atheists many times win debates with religious people is because they point at the weaknesses of the religion at hand. When debating a Christian creationist for example, they can easily show that the Earth was not made in six days – nor six thousand years, depending on the arguer. When debating a Muslim they can easily demonstrate that the moon was never sliced in half, like the Quran suggests. When debating an Hindu or Buddhist, they can disprove the idea of reincarnation and all the flaws and incongruities associated with it. The reality is that religions are full of defects and contradictions that make them easy to target, more often than not leading to their ridicule. But were the atheist to be an integrous, logical and intelligent contender, he would instantly have to address the issue of how ancient, and consequently archaic, religions are – especially the mainstream ones that tend to comprise the primary target of ferocious criticism and persistent diatribes.

Looking back at the history of human knowledge and epistemology, it becomes evident that religion was the starting point of it all. Humans started by looking around and asking questions, amassing the full scope of their understanding at a primeval evolutionary stage within what we today refer to as religion. Whether they were worshiping the sun as a god, trying to use it to migrate to a more hospitable region of the world during the winter, using it as a navigational tool or attempting to grow crops based on the season of the year, all things were encapsulated in the aforementioned concept. Later, accompanying the development of human civilization, philosophy was designed as a means of studying both the physical and metaphysical without necessarily enforcing the works of a particular god or set of gods. Philosophers were naturally mostly religious people but they could communicate inter-religiously when studying different phenomena, even if some times entering in disagreement. Lastly came science, which is nothing more than the detaching of the study of the physical from the metaphysical. In fact it was once part of philosophy under the *natural philosophy* category, and it has always been a tool intentionally configured to solely address physical issues, hence its entire reliance on empirical data.

One could use a *Russian dolls* analogy, where the largest doll represents religion, inside it there is a smaller doll that represents philosophy and, finally, an even smaller doll within it that corresponds to science. Religion takes precedence over both, so it naturally will suffer from the largest amount of inaccuracies due being around for so long, especially at the early stages of human development. Science benefits the most of all three because it only came to be very recently, a little more than a couple of hundreds of years ago or so. It has the huge upper-hand of not being associated with the mistakes of its predecessors, while profiting from all the ideas, theories, and conclusions they got right while avoiding the ones they got wrong. It also benefits greatly from the advantage of not having archaic or obsolete practices and events connected to it.

Religion came first so it's easier to criticize and put down, whereas the field of science did not exist and thereby wasn't used at all, giving it a false sense of grandeur it does not deserve. It's easier to criticize or mock an elderly person for not being good with modern technology but without their presence and contributions we would not be at all, let alone make usufruct of the legacy that was bestowed upon us. As one of the Ten Commandments says (Exodus 20:12) "Honor your father and your mother, so that your days may be prolonged on the land which the Lord has given you."

FOUR THOUSAND GODS

many is better than one

Each of the three forms of pursuit of human knowledge – religion, philosophy and science – has their own place and they are not mutually exclusive, but the atheist will pitch them against one another, suggesting the needlessness of the first two. In fact philosophy may be seen as the function of pointless pursuit of the invisible and non-existent, thence imaginary laws and realms, but religion is the one constituting the major problem. If there is indeed such a thing as deities, or whatever other definition of God is presented, then what solution is true? An age old question, which god out of so many?

During debate, atheists often use this argument to disprove the likelihood of God, because following one of His interpretations would inevitably, and directly, invalidate all others. So if a god is true, which one of them is it? The truth is a multitude of solutions to a problem does in fact reinforce the likelihood of a positive outcome, not the opposite. A strong example is *quantum mechanics.* Scientists working in this field have supplied us with over a dozen interpretations on the theory – should we then follow the atheist's logic and assume this field to be nonsense? If quantum theory is to be taken seriously, which interpretation is correct? Obviously, the more the interpretations, the more likely it is they will eventually lead to an answer. As such, can't one apply the same logic to the interpretation of God? Certainly it appears to not be an option to the atheist.

A battalion of solutions is favorable to the existence of God, justifying a large amount of religions furnishing different cultures with different view points on the subject. It's the lack of gods that should worry the religious, and allow the atheist to take aim at them due to this evolutionary inconsistency. Various cultures will see things in a wide variety of ways, just as two astronomers, one sitting in the southern hemisphere and the other in the northern one, while studying the night sky will come up with different star charts and constellations if they are to observe it concurrently. Is one to deprehend they are observing a different universe, a separate celestial reality? They are simply perceiving different points of view of the same subject, that is the cosmos that surrounds our globe from every direction.

In conclusion, even if atheists present the argument that there are over four thousand gods alive and dead, including those from deceased religions, under the false pretense it makes choosing one religion alone brittle, it can be turned upside-down to actually reflect strength. At the end of the day humans *need* God, and have been searching for answers for millennia, something that would be unrequited were He to be a fabrication of the mind. If not all humans invented the wheel, nor even written languages, how would all of us be able to invent God? What predicament would force us into figuring out one thing over the other? It stands to reason such a global, and ancient, phenomenon is plainly the manifestation of spiritual experiences that need to be addressed and understood, bringing about the need for theories, doctrines and laws that could not otherwise be extracted from the physical universe.

RELIGIOUS LITERALISM

it's not what it says on the tin

Criticism of religion coming from the atheist camp, often resorts to religious literalism, i.e. the need to interpret in a literal manner what is written in scripture. If it's true some religions require a more strict reading of their sacred text, that is surely not the case with most of them – certainly not Christianity. The first book of the Bible, the book of Genesis which was authored by Moses along with four others, takes into account events that were carried forward for thousands of years using the art of *oral tradition*, a method where the history, traditions or culture of a particular group is passed down by word of mouth, one generation to the next, without any chronicles made in written form.

If for Christians, or some of them, there is use for a literal understanding of the Scripture, to the atheist that is definitely not the case. The example of the world being created in six days, or six thousand years taking into consideration other Biblical verses, does not require a direct reading as such. Instead it's easy to deduce this idea can be seen as a metaphor and could also be seen as a symbolism since God doesn't wear a watch. He is not bound by time since His act of Creation allowed both space and time to exist. This determination is so easy to make, even a child could do it, making it clear the need, or better the *want,* for atheists to take in the version that accommodates them the most in a nefarious way so they can loudly justify the wrongness of religion.

Other events like the parting of the waters when the Israelites left Egypt as described in the book of Exodus; the tale of Daniel thrown into the lions' den in his eponymous book; Noah's Ark in the book of Genesis; the books of Job and Jonah with trials and whales respectively; all can be understood as carrying symbolical meanings and messages that this faith's followers can relate to in a very personal and intimate manner. One of the most beautiful traits of the Bible is, due to not being a book but a collection of them, it displays a growing maturity of the way God interacts with His subjects, as the whole compilation was written across a time span of seventeen-hundred years or so.

Atheists love pointing out how harsh the God of the Bible is by using the older texts out of convenience, when they could just come to grips those books, especially the ones written by Moses, refer to a time period when mankind was much more immature, thus making it extremely unfair and disingenuous to use them as a source for diatribes against this religion. It's not that none of what those books contain is useful, but rather that many of the ideas matured and were superseded by better ones, rendering the original ones obsolete. After all, were one to be just, where were atheists during this whole process?

The fact is it would be impossible to prove all Christian denominations wrong, because they contain diverse doctrines based on different viewpoints on the translations of the sacred writings of the Bible, and it would become a mammoth job, if not endless, to carry out. The same pattern would have to then be applied to all religions available, reason why atheists take the easy way out and just dumb everything down as 'silly' or 'magic'. But if this is the case, how come atheists still hold on to so many doctrines and norms they clumsily try to rip-off and pass as their own – or to a certain degree endeavor to validate?

PASCAL'S WAGER

to have or not to have

At dusk of the Renaissance period in Europe, French philosopher and mathematician Blaise Pascal (1623 – 1662 A.D.) proposed a theological argument in the form of a wager, with the intent to expose the inadequacy of using logic and reason when trying to prove or disprove the existence of God. The wager itself contended that if one were to belief in God, if such proposition materialized he would have been rewarded with the infinite grace of living in Heaven, whereas if it turned out to be false the loss, which would relate to hedonistic pleasures, would be finite. Conversely, if one is to choose to *not* believe in God, the punishment of being thrown into the pits of Hell would severely outweigh the pleasures of a life devoted to the whims of the body. To put it simply, is having God better than having no God?

The naysayers, through their typical and incessant atheistic negativity, will try to discredit the wager by introducing a multitude of problems. The evolutionary biologist Richard Dawkins brought up the fact that one could potentially feign belief, while not fully realizing it in their own heart – but does this not suggest full belief? Why go through life making an effort to please God, when not truly holding a belief? It doesn't stand to reason anyone would sacrifice so much for so little. The Australian philosopher John Leslie Mackie (1917 – 1981 A.D.) questioned whether the God that accepted the wage could be the Christian one, Muslim or any other, and as such why choose one at all? A solution for this is presented in the future topic of this very chapter that addresses the spiritual guide. Additionally, the French writer and philosopher Voltaire (1694 – 1778 A.D.) questioned whether God, whichever one, would accept the wage at all, hence not fulfilling it in case of it being a one-sided affair. But is that side of the bargain something we are to worry about? We extrapolate God to represent any good, kindness, honesty and love we can sense, so surely He would not disappoint or forfeit? And if this God is treacherous, should we not follow another? Further, isn't the whole generalization of God as a supreme Creator that of the one true Father? If the thought is to doubt God, surely the disquiet would lead to the assumption he's actually the devil – or something similar not worth trusting. Only the worship of the one and true God is deserving of devotion, which demands all doubt to be thrown out as per what our spiritual sensory inputs inform us of.

It must be noted the wager brought over by the French philosopher did not concern itself with converting someone to a particular faith, or any faith at all. Instead it was unveiling that the pursuit of truth where God is involved relates in no way to a rational process, which is unfortunately something a lot of philosophers and scientists concentrate on. This opens the door to a means of being theistic without necessarily being religious, a prospect that atheists seem to avoid at all costs. Were an individual to choose to embrace the belief in God without affiliating himself to any religion or specific spiritual exegesis, that would still enroll him in the 'theism' category.

In conclusion, is Pascal's Wager proving 'yes' is better than 'no' when applying for an entry to Heaven? The only answer is, at the very least the wager clearly shows that the *ought to do what is good* leads you to Heaven, hence being spirituality objective and beneficial. A believer has a clear advantage over the non-believer or false believer, as hope in reaching a higher state of existence is much greater than the worship of nothingness, and the subsequent mandatory dirge.

AGGRIPA'S TRILEMMA

four is less than three

Epistemology, the arm of philosophy that studies the nature of knowledge, requires postulates or assumptions to be made so as to attain sound conclusions about any of its disciplines, including abstract ones such as mathematics. A trilemma presented by an Ancient Greek philosopher from the first century BC named Agrippa, offers three arguments as the foundation of any knowledge. First the dogmatic, then the circular and finally the regressive, as per **Figure 27**. They all represent logical fallacies, thus proposing that it is impossible for humans to reach the absolute truth regarding anything studied – conclusion this book already agreed with in the previous chapter that discussed the regulatory ideal.

Atheists find comfort in this as it enables their view that pure noesis (intellectual resolve) is in the eye of the beholder – the bearer of thought. This solipsistic approach can accordingly support the meaninglessness of life, or if preferred the God delusion – that is, the emptiness of existence. But in complete contrast, they also frenetically rush to claim that meaning, love or God (as in the source of everything) can be found somewhere else, making them seem like children that rejected their mother's nipple, only to drink from the bottle. A quadrilemma kicks in and the offerings to the gods of atheism are those of the conjugation of *creating* and *preferring*: if the meaning of life is not exogenous, and thus not acquirable, then we are to 'create' it, whatever that means in the vocabulary of atheist orthodoxy. When presented the question "Why is there something rather than nothing?", God as the source of all things is replaced by notional terms such as *beauty* or *because*. There is no verdict, instead just diffusion into the unknown, the unanswerable.

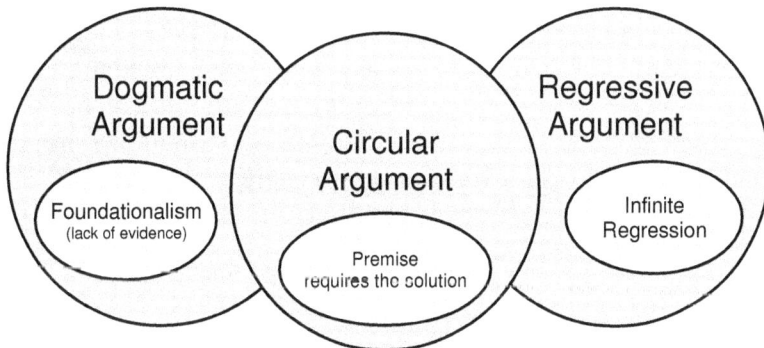

Figure 27: The Aggripan trilemma

Can humans 'create' out of nothing? Are we gods? The Alpha and the Omega gives us just that – a beginning and an ending. Creation is the work of an infinite being that is beyond our comprehension. Any other option leads us into infinite regression, dogmatic truths and circular reasoning. The proposed atheist's quadrilemma is but a refactored version of the original trilemma with a fictional, fabricated extra – a corollary for deniers. Where there is the illusion of a forth solution to escape the limitations of the original three, there is the misconception of something new and alternative. If dogma, regression and circularity do not work, then maybe a shrug allied with the habitual claim "There is no meaning to life at all" might do the trick. However disbelievers keep behaving as if *there is*.

Humans cannot live without hope, as that is what gets us out of bed every morning. The hope to achieve goals, to realize dreams, to fulfill aspirations. To graduate, to marry, to pursue a career, to discover something new, to have one's own child in their arms, to grow as a human being and contribute something towards our species. Without it, all there is left is the dreary reality of being part of a whole bunch of nothing – a large universe devoid of any meaning or purpose. The one true forth option is to accept the trilemma as part of the human condition and hand over the responsibility of carrying any higher burden we can't comport to the only entity that can – the God almighty, creator of all things.

THE NEED FOR OBJECTIVITY

relatively absolute

If all religions have made up their own gods, and thus none of these actually exists, certainly atheism should be able to offer prescriptions and decrees to why humans need to find resolution in aspects of society or personal life. Subjects like ethical norms, love, compassion, human value, etc. are all things that should be either justified without resorting to gods or supernatural phenomena, or be discarded altogether. Faux-atheists reject the latter option, in fact that is why they are *faux* in first place – they need to hold on to practices developed by religious humans without being able to justify them. History tells us that humans don't achieve great results when abandoning these values and concepts, such as communist countries surpassing a death-toll of over one hundred million people in the twentieth century alone.

Taking the natural, historical and evolutionary approach of assuming that humans do require normative ethics to regulate human behavior in order for their societies to strive, it stands to reason that these can be either objective or subjective. If they are subjective, like faux-atheists are forced to suggest because there is nothing in the laws of nature to justify humanism and the sort, then they depend on opinion and preference. If spirituality is simply a state of mind, that can be redefined and re-engineered according to new societal models as needed, then it leaves the door open to interpretation, also known as moral relativism.

Humans, however, do have the inbuilt need for absolutes. Take the *up* and *down* absolutes, where the sky is up and the ground is down, but all these are relative. If one found himself in the middle of the vast, empty space, surrounded by stars in the distance against the pitch-black vacuum and without any reference point, there would be no such definitions as *up* and *down*. Human existence depends on this spacial awareness and an individual's environment is impossible to rationalize without these concepts, proving them to be part of the human condition. We simply can't brush them aside. *Up* and *down* are human absolutes and it's not possible to disregard or neglect them, as similarly there is the need for spiritual and moral values.

Considering moral *good* and *evil* as exogenous to the human mind, i.e. they preexist human beings and exist outside and irrespective of our own existence, we find ourselves a set of objective, absolute flaws and virtues, bad qualities and good ones. Historical results, based on which religion is applied to each civilization, should then be used as a standard to measure these spiritual laws, supplying ours species with objective evidence of whether a religion moves along the path of an absolute, ethereal *Truth,* or if it's the exact opposite.

If these were not laws but instead preferences, there should be an inter-mixture of positive and negative results despite of how *good* or *evil* are defined by each set of norms, of whether to preserve love bonds or not, of whether to consider individual value or snub them. Atheists should at the very least procure to implement a variation (or a combination) of these formulas expecting positive results in more than one instance, instead of falling victim to adopting the rules based on religious doctrine of the gods they preemptively rejected, only to then slap a label on it to make it appear as their own.

A SPIRITUAL GUIDE

not where you are but where you're heading to

Religions should be perceived as paths to the ethereal, metaphysical *Truth.* They are not said *Truth* in themselves, neither do they own it. Considering the sciences of Alchemy and Chemistry: not only one led to the other but they both achieved results that were useful towards scientific improvements. Chemistry is undoubtedly the most successful of the two, to the point of the former being cast-off completely in the modern age of science and technology, because not only it is much more accurate and complete but it also gives us greater detail in how to understand nature and the cosmos at a microscopic level. Why keep a more deficient science if the other achieves superior results? It would be plain imbecilic and redundant to do so.

The object of religion is not the study of molecular structures or atomic ones, radiation or the reaction of chemicals when mixed together, focusing instead in answering questions that move humans away from their primordial state of existence. We are born being creatures inserted into a natural environment offered to us by Mother Nature. We are therefore to conform with the rules of the animal kingdom. But somehow we seem to have gone farther and escaped them to a particular degree. We reassessed ourselves as more than just autonomous living organisms, processing food and reproducing without any other sense of purpose, and found a way to bring meaning into our own existence. Religion is the guide to the laws of the spiritual world that drive us away from animality (**Figure 28**). The more any specific religion moves us towards the latter instead of the former, the less we obey our soul and the more we obey our body.

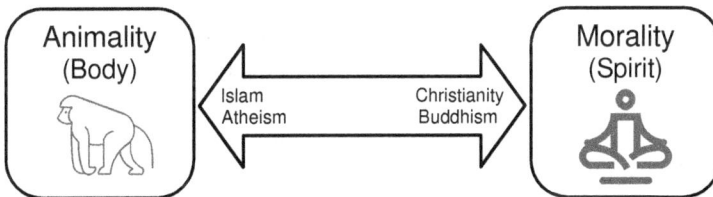

Figure 28: The dual nature of worship

The God of the Bible for instance, the Alpha and the Omega,

the beginning and the ending, far outmatchs the petty, anthropomorphic gods of the Olympus, and most gods of dead religions alike. As it stands today, Christianity achieved unfathomably the most astounding results in terms of pushing civilization forward, with a clear and inextricable link to the human behavioral norms deeply-rooted in this religion. If one moves towards the divine then abstract concepts and ideas such as *beauty, moral good, love, integrity, honour, kindness, compassion, altruism,* etc. become accepted as sacred laws that, albeit not being found in the physical realm, supplant any laws of the animal kingdom – the ones that our physical body is bound to and persistently try to bring us into submission.

The success of each religion should thereby be measured not just in scientific, technological and medical advancements, which come as byproduct and are thus secondary to religious practice, but in how synergistic, cooperative and harmonious people are when operating within that societal model. If God is the *Truth*, then He is the *N* marked in the compass (see **Figure 29**), representing north. Each religion is a needle in the same compass, its success deriving from how much it aligns with the mark of absolute, divine *Truth*. A religion that focuses on truthful spiritual guidance will achieve superiors results, just like Chemistry does over Alchemy, because embracing the truth leads invariably to success. If on the other hand a religion is focused on carnal, material, power-hungry, egotistical affairs, it shall fail as it clenched onto the path of an inferior truth – that is the path towards animality and mechanicity, resolving into a backwards, primitive societal state. If pledging to the atheist god of worshiping the void, all bets are off and it's a free for all scenario. With no acceptance of any metaphysical truth, nothing can be made forbidden under such spiritual vacuum.

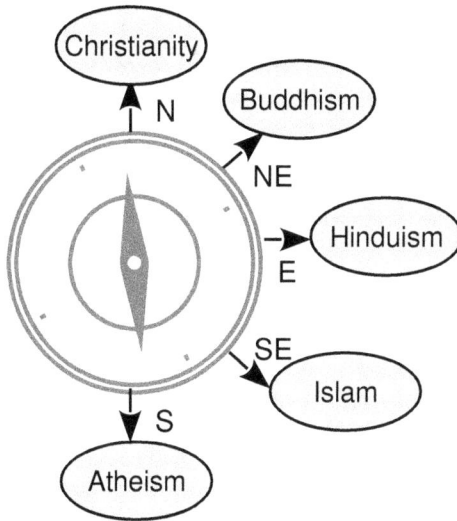

Figure 29: The spiritual compass

It's best to look at the endpoint of a religion, or what light at the end of the tunnel there is, if any, and how dim it appears to be. A religion should not be judged solely by its past achievements, or lack thereof, but also the displayed potential of where it could lead us to. Moving one step forward towards the light is the primary objective, towards infinity since the light itself is unreachable by us – and that's a good thing. If we cannot have Heaven on Earth, we can at least move in its general direction to the best of our efforts, whereas reverting back to being cave dwellers will hardly present a challenge. In John 14:6 Jesus said "I am the way, the truth and the life", and indeed the path towards the *Truth* allowed us humans to truly experience life, discover, understand, innovate and self-improve, bringing us all the way to the modern, free world.

CHAPTER 6

Teapots and Unicorns

A FALSE EQUIVALENCE

cornucopia

Santa Claus, the Tooth-fairy, the Easter Bunny and other folklore have very frequently been used by faux-atheism evangelists in order to draw comparisons to religious figures, or even the simple act of holding any positive faith when it comes to the metaphysical. Through derision and mockery, they liken Moses to Santa, Buddha to the tooth-fairy, Shiva or any others to leprechauns and such. The idea of escaping the claws of empirical knowledge, of neglecting the information the body delivers to us through the its five senses in favor of spiritual Gnosis, is to these new atheists a death sentence in terms of logic and reason. On their hands religion falls into ridicule under the guise of intellectual superiority. They don't need to resort to fables or magic as a means to evade their fears of non-existence, nor do they struggle to find fulfillment in their beingness.

All things immaterial are marked accordingly as 'silly' or 'childish', as they are well above needing such petty beliefs to embrace life and live it to its fullest. But not all is well in the kingdom of the faux-atheist, since these reputed masters of reason and advocates of science fail to see the devil is in the details – or lack there of. If one were to make a theoretical experiment in the realm of music, proceeding as such: if there were three individuals who presented themselves as Classical Music experts, and they were given five pieces to listen to as follows:

- Ludwig van Beethoven's Symphony No 5
- Gustav Holst's The Planets
- Carl Orff's Carmina Burana
- Metallica's Enter Sandman
- Britney Spears' Baby One More Time

If the first contender claimed all are the same and belong to the same category, because in the end it's all music, certainly he would be discarded immediately. If the second challenger could tell the difference between Heavy Metal, Pop and Classical Music but was unable to distinguish which of the first three pieces were by which composer, he would follow suit and his application also binned as a consequence. Finally, if the remaining candidate were able to identify each of the classical pieces by author, even if he wasn't familiar with last two extraneous pieces he listened to, clearly thrown in for confusion, he would surely be the only one to qualify as a true expert in this music field. Behind this simple analogy is the fact that possessing a coarser understanding on any special subject is detrimental to those speaking about it.

Taking into consideration the example of the *ethereal teapot*, which is a common atheist trope utilized to discredit religious beliefs as senseless, where the proposed idea is: if there were an ethereal teapot orbiting planet Saturn, would one necessarily believe in it? It won't make any difference, because no one can witness it, touch it (since it's immaterial), nor perceive it in any way shape of form – literally. So the issue presented would be, why believe in something that isn't tangible, and therefore will never be proven to exist? The simple answer, were atheists true people of reason and engaged in critical thinking as many of them purport to be, is that this ethereal teapot would have no purpose, as its nature would be superfluous and pointless, and would affect no one in any way, irrespective of it *being* or not. The existence of God on the other hand, gives us hope, a purpose and validates morality, love and other things the material universe and its laws cannot offer judgment on. The teapot, were it to exist, is completely irrelevant to define our behavior and perspective on life, when on the diametrical opposite side of this pointlessness is God – rendering the similitude entirely fabricated, but sure serves as a good distraction to pretend a valid argument has been formulated in a cogitative manner.

The folklore is then brought in by atheists, especially of the *faux* kind, to distract from the fact they have nothing – nothing at all – when it comes to objective justifications and explanations pertaining what religion affords to fairly easily explicate. Santa, the tooth-fairy, unicorns and such are trivial when compared to religion, and only someone with a coarse, rough, perhaps even obtuse, view on the subject would reach this type of conclusion – just like a person with no knowledge of classical music trying to pass as an expert. If one isn't able to make a discernment based on the clean-cut detailed information available, only ignorance or malice are left to warrant such behavior. Religion is not equivalent even remotely to fables or folklore, as the these are presented as stories to children with little to no meaning, other than the one to make them fall asleep or keep them optimistic when preparing them for the long journey ahead in this very often unpleasant world.

It's actually the faux-atheists that transform science and reason into their adult playground as opposed to religious people, given the farcical, incongruous arguments they bring over in good measure. Trapped in their cage of darkness and emptiness, lacking a superlative entity they can relay such burden to, they often offer simple solutions for a complex truth. The theory of a universe from nothing is a prime example, where they are met with the dead-end of not being able to investigate *nothingness* and some preferring to twist it into *something*, such as quantum fluctuations (also known as vacuum fluctuations), which can hardly be qualified as nothing. Others take their intentions into a more mathematical hypothesis called the *zero-energy universe*, where they limit themselves to proposing the idea that if the total amount of energy in the universe amounts to exactly zero, they would have a state of "a universe from nothingness" – an absolute blunder in the making, since this would only prove, like any logical person would expect, that before the universe existed, there wasn't any universe. This does not confirm the idea there is nothing outside or before the universe, at all since it's a *non-sequitur*. These are truly childish incursions of atheists desperately trying to prove their faith correct, often butchering scientific theory in their rushing stampede into the dark, empty abyss of death they revere as god.

Even a *Creatio ex nihilo* (a creation out of nothing) would still allow for God to exist within that nothingness, as the definition of the latter would only encompass the absence of space and time, not *nihilo ominous* – the dreary, unconditioned void; the empty, utter darkness of absolute nonexistence.

THE EXISTENTIAL AXIOM

God is, therefore I am

Science is in actuality inadequate to prove or disprove spirituality. The acceptance of God is based on faith, thence the twofold *yes* or *no* answer when handling matters that transcend our empirical abilities. If reason is the tool we use to tell truth from falsehood, as rational creatures we can apply this methodology to the abstract thought without relying perforce in experience or observation. Mathematics is a great example of a field of study where conscious intellectual exercise can operate without the need to resort to factual knowledge. However, even in such fields there is the need for axioms, that is to say self-evident truths that are recognized as absolute, incontrovertible rules that cannot be broken, otherwise the whole system collapses on itself.

Human absolutes can vary from innate notions such as *up*, *down*, *left and right*, *light* and *dark*, *true* and *false*, *positive* and *negative*, *one* is different from *zero*, and so on and so forth, not all of them binary but all inescapably universal. If one were to reject these concepts, communication would reveal itself to be impossible, as reason is grounded in logic, which is nothing more than a set of axioms used to configure formal principles for reason and, by extension, rationality (pure abstract thought). This bounds humans to their own condition of explaining reality, material or otherwise, under the burden of their limited intellects. The absolute truth would dictate *up* and *down* to not exist, just like *red*, *green* and *blue* neither, other than within our human minds, or our subjective, shared point of view of experience.

A straightforward way of demonstrating the need for axioms is by looking at the phenomenon of *pareidolia*: the false perception of meaningful patterns or shapes where in fact there are none, solely randomness instead. For example, like when someone sees clouds shaped like a bunny or a sheep, or maybe a face carved in the tree bark. A more recent manifestation of this phenomenon is what one could call *chat-bot pareidolia*, where humans interact with a computer program, conveying the sense of an intelligent being that understands or acts like one of us. This A.I. (Artificial Intelligence) simulators transmit to the end user an illusion of personality, preference, choice and, more importantly, consciousness. But an experienced computer software engineer with a long career working in low-level fields of computing, where the software meets the hardware (the heart of the device where assembly language, registers and machine-code, among other things can be found) can attest for the impossibility for a machine, no matter how complex it may become, to turn conscious. Computers are at their core made of transistors, billions of them, that can be seen, in an extremely simplistic manner, as *on* and *off* switches. There is nothing sentient about a machine, and there never will be.

This takes one deep into the ontology, or the study of being, of life itself, what existence is and how that reflects onto us humans. To give atheists a chance, were we to assume, like they do, humans to be molecular structures with no meaning or purpose, indeed just a byproduct of a universe in constant change and under great tension between its laws and the fabric of space and time, the end result would dictate sentience and consciousness to be just an illusion. But this 'solution' introduces a new problem – a very serious one: by removing the ethereal part out of the human being, the only thing that is left is matter. In effect this reduces human existence to that of a machine. It could be said man and computer (an A.I. chat-bot) are made of the same *stuff*. The inexorable, unavoidable conclusion is that humans aren't conscious either, nor are they sentient. Failing to 'upgrade' computers to the level of humans, atheists simply *downgrade* humans to machines. This, needless to say, changes nothing, since the illusion of consciousness is still there and if one is to accept anything as human absolutes, without which an individual can't function, the axioms must be brought into place.

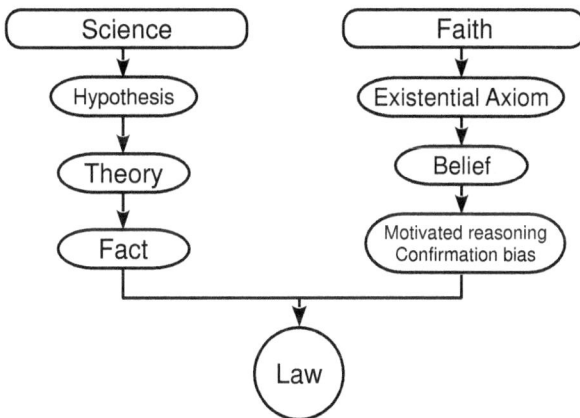

Figure 30: Scientific method vs faith

If Pascal's Wager attempted to seduce its wagers to embrace God out of the beneficial outcome it would bring them, maybe we should instead simply humbly prostate ourselves to the primary, imperative and fundamental existential axiom – God. The solution is the act of reducing ourselves to our insignificance so we can reach human truths, i.e. truths that aren't absolute in themselves but are as far and deep the human mind can hope to cognize.

COMPLEXITY, HUBRIS AND RANDOMNESS

all I know is, I know everything

With the vast improvement of human knowledge through scientific achievements, advancements in technological, communication and information, plus medical breakthroughs, arrogance and smugness became dominant in modern societies, especially the First World ones. The rise in the adoption of atheistic views and beliefs is tightly tied to this negative change, as cognitive bias led these societies to toss out the need for a superior, supreme being – an omniscient overseer that could offer explanations too complex for humans to comprehend. At the end of the day, if mankind can figure things out on its own, why the need to resort to an invisible entity when looking for answers?

Enter the *Dunning-Kruger effect*, that pertains to the idea of an individual overestimating their understanding of a particular subject matter, based on poor self-awareness, weak general knowledge or deficient cognitive ability. In practice, people that have no knowledge of any particular subject might refrain from opinionating on it, but once they acquire a mild knowledge more often than not perceive themselves, albeit incorrectly, as mighty experts – or they simply just dumb down the field they operate on to fit their bias or predilection. When applying this effect at large (as per **Figure 31**), one could classify it as *civilizational Dunning-Kruger effect*, which translates into the false perception of humanity of having acquired enough knowledge to the extent it can work out all solutions on its own. This can also be substantiated by the vertiginous dive into modernity, including exposure to a multitude of cultures that used to be self-contained; the ability to communicate with anyone around the world in an immediate manner using the internet or mobile phone technology; the power to amass knowledge of world events in an almost simultaneous instance through news broadcast, especially when it comes to catastrophes, cataclysms and wars. The human intellect and psyche are simply not ready for the earthshaking impact of so many new changes occurring at such a rapid pace, producing nefarious mass formation outcomes such as hysteria, delusion, dysfunction, psychosis and hubris.

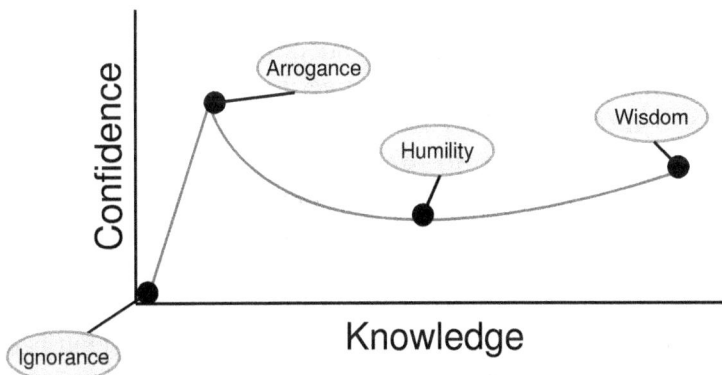

Figure 31: Civilizational Dunning-Kruger effect

There is a large increase in people that detach themselves from spiritual notions and thus enlist in the ranks of atheism, finding solace in supposedly scientific 'solutions' that come short of satisfying their emotional and behavioral needs. But this belief that humans can fully grasp absolute truths, i.e. the truth as *it is* and not as we *see it*, can lead to extremely incorrect assumptions. These happens even outside the social element, sometimes in scientific fields that relate little to no way to human psychology or conduct. Some molecular biologists argue against a *theory of evolution* that would require more than the 4.28 billion years suggested for the age of the planet we inhabit – with this estimate being in the higher range. A more reasonable approximation would lead it to drop to at least 3.77 billion years, which would make the whole evolutionary process even more difficult to uphold. The lesser time life has been on the planet, the less likelihood of the theory not requiring an exogenous factor, making its authentication a remote possibility. For living organism to sprawl into such degree of complexity and variety, these biologists claim quite a few more billion years would be required for planet Earth to acquire such enrichment in terms of biodiversity.

Some obtuse, atheist defenders of Darwinism, the ones that claim it's not a theory any longer but actual fact, zealously protect it through faith. This regardless of the giant gaps and inconsistencies in macro evolution which result in many missing links for the theory's completion into scientific fact. These problems do not defeat or undo the triumphs of the theory itself, but they do prove how the atheist's presumptuousness rushes them into the precipice – the atheist doesn't really care about the truth or science, but instead needs desperately to justify his biased faith under any circumstances, no matter what cost. The theory of *intelligent design* could be refactored to be simply seen as the influence of a metaphysical dimension into the process of molding complex living organisms, thus accelerating their composition without resorting to magic formulas – and allowing the current estimates to reflect an extreme abundance of time.

Another absurdity that can be found on the atheist camp is the idea that at heart, and based on the uncertainty principle, the universe is random. The study of Quantum Mechanics has proven itself to be the most difficult scientific field to plunge into, if only because we humans are constricted to only use the smallest things the universe is made of – elementary particles – to study their own behavior, and what they effectively are. This constitutes an irreducibly difficult challenge because scientists cannot slice these particles the way one would slice an apple in order to see what's inside – and what components they are made of, if anything at all. A very simplistic way of discerning the problem is with a pool table analogy: imagining that a blindfolded player can only determine the position of an ever-moving black ball by throwing the white ball at it, with the contact implicating finding *where* the black ball is or *when* it was, thus its location or its speed can be resolved in a mutually exclusive approach. The action itself will dislodge the position of the black ball, leading to the uncertainty of its new state.

No matter what the human fundamental limits are in terms of accuracy in the field of Quantum Mechanics or how imprecise the methodologies applied are, the truth of the matter is we can rationalize the notion of *probability*, *uncertainty* and *randomness* to the effect these three definitions are all related to the limitations of the human intellect, as opposed to properties or laws that exist within the universe and govern it. If drawing a comparison with an asteroid that is moving towards the Earth, when asking a NASA astronomer the odds of it hitting our planet the following responses can be played with: if his answer is 50/50, then we consider him useless since we could have ascertained that ourselves, as it reflects the complete lack of any further information regarding the matter; if, on the other hand, he gives us a decent probability of 10% of hitting our planet, we can be relaxed as the likelihood is low, assuming the astronomer engaged in due diligence and reached that figure using empirical data not accessible to common people, this way reducing his uncertainty about the event.

The natural conclusion is *probability* isn't real, but instead a subjective simplification of the human mind due to the inaccurate prediction on different phenomena. If the astronomer gives us a 0% change of the asteroid hitting our globe, probability has been totally removed out of the equation based on investigation. Nevertheless, some scientists devote all their lives and careers defending these type of scientific abominations, such as the theory of a universe from nothing – all in the name of the non-existence of God they so fervorously advocate for. God sees everything, and therefore there is no uncertainty in His mind but only in the human one. This is another peril of humanity playing god, only to fall clumsily down the spiral of disappointment. No matter how long our species survives, it's unfeasible to project a future where we wholly got rid of any probability whatsoever.

THE NEED FOR THE SOUL

towards the light

Existential nihilism is the rejection of the simple question, why is there something rather than nothing? This philosophical theory renders this inquiry redundant as there is no immanent meaning to life or the value of the individual. Reduced to being parts of a whole, humans are demoted to just comprising of molecular structures that manufacture and concoct their own value through a delusional sense of sentience. Like one of the fiercest advocates of the theory, the French philosopher Jean-Paul Sartre (1905 – 1980 A.D.), said "Existence precedes essence – man first exists, [...] then defines himself afterwards", i.e. we are walking receptacles for the universe to observe itself, only to indulge in a false sense of meaning and identity. This particular perspective on life and human beingness is the stepping stone of post-modernism, with atheism as the driving force behind it.

The belief that God does not exist leads to the withering of the spiritual body, commonly referred to as the soul. Without one there is no light at the end of the tunnel and, as consequence, any fork we take down the road is acceptable and logical. There is no procurement of divinity or any of its associated traits, like beauty, love and righteousness – of the moral kind. Everything becomes diffuse and permissiveness abounds. Rules and regulations can be prescribed and decreed but fall short of being objective and, not being attached to anything, can be questioned, dismantled and reconstructed. We have the need for the soul to explain who we are, otherwise it's a free-for-all and anything's a go. Without this incorporeal body that allows us to perceive this extra set of laws that cannot be found in the space-time universe, the one that bestowed upon us our material reality, it becomes a pointless, fruitless quest to dwell in any teleological matters – why are we here and what is the finality of human existence?

Putting for consideration the possibility that the soul is the point of entry of God into the universe, a connection between our worldly bodies and divine authority is made without the need to resort to any sort of wizardry. If we have an insubstantial presence that gathers information from the ethereal realm, where laws transcendental to science can be found, it's also suitable to conceive that influence in the material realm could be exerted from this very source. This would justify in a satisfactory manner miracles and other otherworldly phenomena that science doesn't understand but the 'bleeding' of such supernatural laws into the natural world would easily vindicate – the sort of occurrence that is usually labeled as *divine intervention*. The traditional *cause-and-effect*, which reduces everything, including human beings, to a function of its cause, could then be regarded solely applicable to the physical universe, and nothing else.

In conclusion, we need the soul not simply to explain why we are and thence earn a sense of purpose, but also to explicate the who and how we are. Rejecting to do so by adopting any form of atheism leaves a lot of questions perpetually unanswered, precipitating us into a life of an unfulfilling, meaningless existence.

UNIVIRTUAL

no place like nowhere

With the advent of computer technology, new theories have emerged to conform with the new ways of thinking in modern society. The idea of the universe we inhabit potentially being a virtual simulation is one of the most popular. Nonetheless, if a bit of thought is put into this the entire construct can be quickly dismantled, to the extent of human truths.

The first argument is that if there are Olympian alien entities running the simulation, and they introduced living organisms to such things as love and compassion, they could not have created these concepts unless they experience them themselves. This leads to a conundrum: if these entities are capable of love and empathy, how would they be capable of creating self-aware entities like ourselves that could feel fear, anguish and existential dread? Whatever exists in the simulation would have to be taken from these superior entities' own experiential realm, as they could not possibly create things from nothing – if they could, then we are simply referring to gods, in which case seems pointless to come up with the theory of our universe being a simulation, but rather accept it as a creation of the gods as defined by religion, rendering this whole concept and theories that argue in its favor redundant.

A second and even stronger argument is that, if we are to be entities that exist solely as part of the simulation, then we are very similar to what we can find in our own human computerized versions. The acronym *NPC* appeared in the computing in the early stages of the video-game industry, referring to the *Non Player Character*, i.e. characters that are controlled fully by the computer simulation, as opposed to the ones that are controlled by the player enjoying the experience. If the universe is indeed virtual, we would only exists as NPCs within it, which brings up a very serious problem. The entities in charge of handling the simulation we live in would be able to mid-simulation, pause, rewind, frame-skip, etc. any events, just like it happens on a DVD. Unlike with the movie *The Matrix* (1999), no-one would be able to step out of this virtual world or see any glitches, since the mighty overseers of the virtual universe would have full power over any occurrences we underwent, fixing any problems or issues as needed. If a human had indeed witness a glitch, the simulation engineers would fix it, rewind time and all memories of that individual would be rewound with it.

It's literally impossible to 'discover' that the universe isn't real, unless the creators of this virtual reality we find ourselves in intended for us to do so. We can only be aware of the things we are *allowed* to be aware of, nothing more, nothing less. A simulation is just the recreation of a certain environment imagined by its manufacturers, who will by default, and necessity, have full power to command it as they please. It's not as if the ones going through the experience can do anything about it, as they are fully circumscribed like puppets to the *reality* they were inserted into by vastly superior entities.

One further argument can be presented to reproach those who incur in the fallacy of believing any living organism can grasp the unthinkable and obtain a final answer regarding the universe we inhabit being real or artificially generated. If a superior group of entities created the virtual universe we humans are part of, how can they, themselves, be sure they aren't a creation of an even superlative mind to their own? They would be placed in the exact same conditions as us, since whatever mind or entities created their world would have the power to apply the same restrictions discussed above, when defending the impossibility of finding true resolution regarding this matter. In fact accepting this idea will enforce *infinite regression*, which can be defined as the process of looking into an infinite chain of events while expecting to find answers. Indistinguishable from the famous *Droste* effect it would lead to an endless cycle, like that of a Russian doll inside another Russian doll into infinity. Unless reaching the ultimate entity, the omniscient God, any other entities would be limited to understand only things within their capabilities, their own constrictions and their own truths. Any efforts attempting to find a way beyond their grasp would have to be construed as a mere reflection of arrogance and hubris.

LAPLACE'S DEMON

fateless

The French scholar Pierre-Simon de Laplace (1749 – 1827 A.D.) defended the idea that if there was a super-entity, who he called a *demon,* whom in his omniscience was aware of the precise point in space and moment in time of each particle in the universe, this *demon* could predict every 'slice' of time since the birth of the universe. To this he stated: "We may regard the present state of the universe as the effect of its past and the cause of its future", referring to what was in the French scholar's time *determinism,* but is today labeled *pre-determinism*, which is the idea that everything material has been preordained since the dawn of time. To this effect, rewinding to a previous given moment will always lead to the same timeline, with all universe motions, events and actions (including human ones) being fully fixed to each time slice and immutable – maybe he was a bit ahead of this time since, once more, this is very much like rewinding a movie stored in DVD medium or similar. The only difference between the two theories or views, is that determinism (also known as *causal determinism*) does not concern itself with the predictability of events, that is it does not claim that the future is implicit in the present, thus leaving out the idea of fate.

Recent developments in the field of Quantum

Mechanics, appear to show that, at heart, the universe is governed by uncertainty, leading to the conclusion that randomness plays a major role in its existence, substantiating the idea of *indeterminism*, which lies in the polar opposite of the aforementioned theories. As covered in this very chapter, probability is nothing more than insufficient human knowledge to reach a conclusion about a specific query, making it essentially a product of the human mind, as opposed to something that science can ascertain as 'real'. But even disregarding this truism, one could still easily dismiss the possibility of agency as the factor behind animal (including human) actions, opinions and behavior because even if it turns out the deeper levels of the material world are stochastic, any type of life still operates under the control of the laws of physics, random or not.

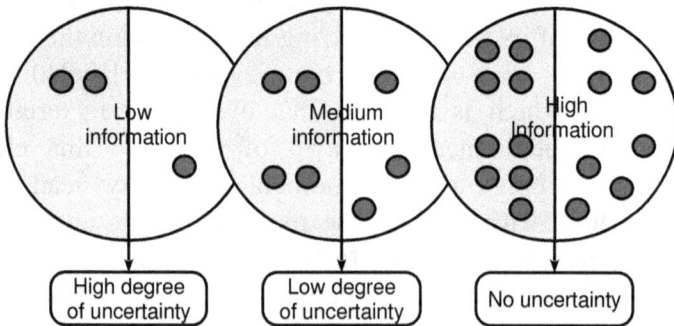

Figure 32: Deterministic (left hemisphere) and Stochastic (right) probability both depend on lack of information

If an individual were to rob a bank, the only difference between the deterministic approach and the indeterministic one, is that when repeating the process, in the former the robber would default to always rob the bank, whereas in the latter the robber would occasionally be 'told', at quantum level within his brain, not to rob it. Without *libertarian freewill*, the robber is not his own actor but simply a puppet in the universe's hands – he will do has he is told irrespective of how that effect (to rob or not to rob) came about. If the demon were to rewind time multiple times, it could be the robber would do the evil deed nine times out of ten due to his miscreant character, even with uncertainty principles thrown in, but there would be no exogenous mind to control the agent, and thence no freewill. The cause of such effect would always be imputed to Quantum Mechanics, independent of any implicated consequences.

BAD SCIENCE

held entirely by belief

The idea of the universe being a simulation, as addressed previously, would lead to the conclusion science would inevitably be testing artificially created laws, turning our efforts pointless, no matter how deep our knowledge of how these laws work. This can expose severe flaws of the atheistic scientific method, as they rely on the following:

1. Postulate the universe is real.
2. Collect empirical data using the senses.
3. Use rational thinking to process the gathered data.
4. Assert only verified information is valid.

Or to use syllogistic logic one could say, the universe is real and studying it allows us to understand reality, therefore science supplies us with the truth. But if the first premise can be put into question, then the statement becomes illogical, or at least doubtful. We don't *know* if the universe is real, we just *presume* so. A healthy dose of skepticism is welcome when engaging in scientific scrutiny, but the same should not be applied to metaphysical matters, as it requires inquiry, investigation and verification. To summarize, skepticism should be fully applied within the scientific field, allowing for the assumption of the verisimilitude of the universe to take place. This will satisfy to its advocates the following postulates of science:

- What can be asserted without evidence can be dismissed without evidence.
- Absence of evidence is not evidence of absence.

But since atheism precludes God and any sort of metaphysics, in order to impose these postulates, they cannot be applied to any inquiry into the spiritual or religious, as they are preceded by the atheist's negative belief. To depend on the scientific method and skepticism to conjecture the non-existence of God is just bad science. Evidently, this does not apply to claims regarding supernatural phenomena made by religious or spiritual people within the realm of material world, which are therefore subject to scientific audit. Whether it relates to speaking with the dead, if the moon was cut in half or how old the universe really is, this type of averment are subject to the above postulates.

If skepticism cannot dwell in metaphysical matters, and neither can science by attachment, then those who claim to have found a solution for the beginning of this realm by conjecturing that the universe came from nothing, it can be said what they are engaging in is nothing more than an abhorrence, of the scientific kind nonetheless. It requires the need to redefine nothing, which is an abstract concept to boot and is irredeemably immutable, turning such idea into something utterly absurd and very much anti-scientific. Without resorting to such trick, how can these supposed scientists gather evidence from *nothing,* when that process requires *something* to probe? Irrespective of the type of *nothing* they present, whether it's the *nihilous ominous* (an absolute nothing) or simply the absence of the natural world, of space and time, in either case they do not concern this universe. Because of this one can only conclude the theory in question constitutes bad science.

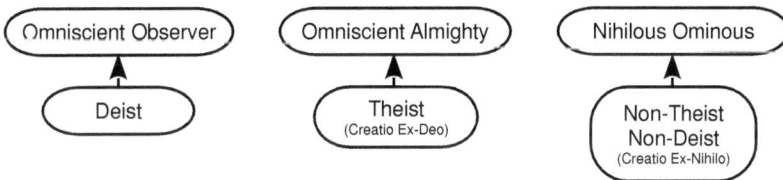

Figure 33: God as the origin of everything

One last note to refer that it's not that Spinoza's god, or the laws of physics as God, is the wrong viewpoint, but it's certainly incomplete, because the word replacement strategy cannot satisfy behavioral questions and conundrums – it offers solely a set of mechanical laws that can't justify all that humans experience and cogitate on. This 'god' is actually only a partial manifestation of the one, true, almighty God, not the totality of Him. If such entity is present everywhere one goes, like the Bible states: (Genesis 28:15) "Behold, I am with you and will keep you wherever you go", then He must permeate the integrality of existence. Any nook and cranny of beingness, including the physical universe, would not exist without God, because without Him only chaos, darkness and emptiness would be left – the *nihilous ominous*.

CHAPTER 7

Science of no Good or Evil

THE THREE PILLARS OF WESTERN VIRTUE

you do not have a soul, you are a soul

Christian Liberal Democracies were founded under the principle of the individual being granted exemption from capricious and oppressive exercise of authority by the state. Three main principles constitute the pillars of Western societies as they are today, which in turn were exported globally to many other regions of the globe. The French flag can often be used as the strongest symbol and most iconic representation of the Western societies biogenic principles for the instauration and development of the modern world. Without Freedoms, Equality and Secularism, such undertaking would not have been possible. In fact these Biblical doctrines are so intimately tied to the French Revolution (1789 – 1799 A.D.) and the American War of Independence (1775 – 1783 A.D.) that the world as we know it would not have anything *modern* about it were these event not have come to pass.

If there is to be a social environment where personal

freedoms abound, a religion that prerequisites a personal relationship with God suits the concept of *individual sovereignty*, since at its heart is the idea of the uniqueness of the being; if such religion calls for equal rights and opportunities, *state sovereignty* will derive from a large contingent of individuals that rejoice in those very freedoms; finally, a fraternity, or better put a guild of an homogeneous collective, where postulates follow a bottom-up design, preventing state dominance and influence from theocratic regimes and the like.

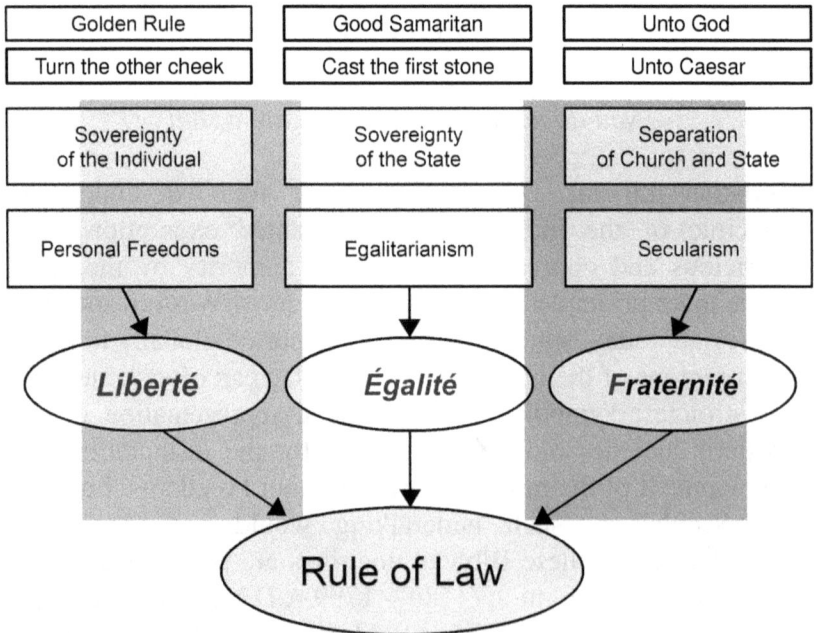

| Golden Rule | Good Samaritan | Unto God |
| Turn the other cheek | Cast the first stone | Unto Caesar |

| Sovereignty of the Individual | Sovereignty of the State | Separation of Church and State |

| Personal Freedoms | Egalitarianism | Secularism |

Liberté   *Égalité*   *Fraternité*

Rule of Law

Figure 34: The three Pillars of Western Virtue (Western Christian Liberal Democracies)

However the Christian *ethos* came under heavy attack in the early and later twentieth century Europe, in two separate instances following both wars, under the post-illuminist atheistic school of thought. The inescapable derailing into degeneracy due to the lack of an cohesive *ethos*, succeeded by the inevitable descent into chaos due to the lack of freedom, took place as the absence of an objective, exogenous *noumenon* left these post-revolutionary societies with an immense spiritual vacuum. Social convulsions persist, especially in the West where a thrid iteration of such 'revolutions' is still ongoing.

At this point a distinction must be made between *morals* and *ethics* instead of using them synonymously. The first refers to the way one uses their judgment, which invariably refers to a subjective, therefore more personal, point of view, inferring values rooted in a spiritual perception, commonly referred to as faith or religious belief. The second relates to the rules and norms of social conduct, grounding itself on the way humans from a particular group interact with each other. In conclusion, *morals* relate to conscience, whereas *ethics* relate to society. Without God, conscience becomes opinion and the collapse of a transcendental *ethos*, under the guise of its replacement with something 'healthier', ensues.

Another distinction between *freedom* and *liberty* must be brought into play. While the former can be defined as the ability for someone to make choices or decisions, and take actions without any interference or impediment, the latter can be described as being a concerted effort of noninvasive freedoms within a societal model. In other words, when operating within society, allowing people to exert full personal freedoms leads to anarchy, because there would be total and complete mutual disregard between fellow constituents. This is blatantly evident in socialist movements that are massively dependent on intolerant methodologies in order to impose the group's will onto the others who oppose them. *Liberty*, on the other hand necessitates a reciprocal, consonant social interrelationship to be built and established, resulting in order and synergy.

The newly formulated atheistic *ethos* is dependent on either an *argument from virtue* or an *argument from convenience*. In the first, the self-proclaimed revolutionary virtuoso creates its own rules at leisure – but what is virtue if not their own imagination and delusion? The absence of an object to extract the rules from, similar to the way we observe laws within the universe, leaves the new ethical norms as purely prescriptive or declarative. As to the second there isn't much difference, other than preference takes over, usually in order to privilege the collective the revolutionary belongs to, thence suffering from the same pitfalls as the previous argument. Intellectual indolence is a convenience factor for the latter arrangement, since it's possible to avoid pursuing all possible avenues of investigation and saving themselves a lot of hard-work and effort. A little like that of an incompetent police force running an investigation and using motivated reasoning by deciding, preemptively and by choice, the husband is guilty in order to retro-fit any available evidence and lazily throw away everything else.

EUSOCIAL TOTALITARIANISM

an antless ant-farm

It's healthy to find skepticism at the core of the modern view of the world, as it enforces an inquisitive attitude for the benefit of acquiring knowledge through a process that involves doubt and uncertainty. However when applying this strategy outside the scientific realm, like atheists do, it becomes useless and deformative. Skepticism cannot put into question things that are not seen, that which is intangible and therefore lies outside the grasp of scientific examination. This noesis, in the Platonic sense, can only be appreciated by an immaterial source, or a spiritual body that the atheist declares not to exist, coinciding with the famous Biblical verses (John 20:29) "Blessed are the ones who have not seen and yet have believed" and (Mathew 4:4) "Man shall not live on bread alone, but on every word that proceeds out of the mouth of God.". That is to say, humans need more then the basic information who's provinience is their material body in order to understand themselves.

Neglecting the soul, humans started refactoring their view of society and the role they possess in their own civilization. The individual's importance was relegated to second place, with society at the helm. The Christian *ethos* of approaching society from inside-outwards, i.e. first comes the individual and society is but a collection of rights and principles applied to them, was reversed with the *whole* taking precedence of its *parts*. This atheistic phenomenon we shall denote by the term *eusocial totalitarianism* (**Figure 35**): a philosophical system in which the individual is integrated like a cog in a machine, becoming just another square in a grid, where all squares share the same exactness. The latter is prioritized over the former, resulting in a mechanistic societal mold that inescapably dehumanizes and depreciates people in the pursuit of meaningless civilizational progress and advancement. A purely reductivist approach, fully antagonistic to the previous Christian ethos that dominated Western culture for centuries, and all the successes and improvements associated with it.

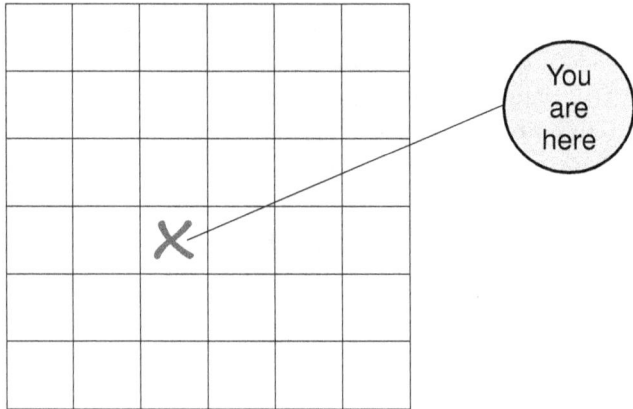

Figure 35: Philosophical Totalitarianism (Human ant-colony model)

The proliferation of this system occurred due to the philosophical current of Existentialism earning an abundance of atheist followers, first with the German philosopher Friedrich Nietzsche (1844 – 1900 A.D.) and his alert to the disintegration of Christian morality and traditional Western values, introducing the concept of the *Übermensch* and his *master-slave* moral dynamics, which inevitably spawned the idea of *eugenics*. Even though it contrasted with the Marxist appeal to *dysgenics* and its focus on the masses, both of these ideological instruments perfectly fit the eusocial totalitarian system, where humanity is reduced to a human ant-colony model under complete servitude to the oppressive and despotic *whole*. It stands to reason that the nineteenth century industrial European landscape would prove the be the utopian breeding ground for this type of narrow-focused, spiritually impaired, but prolific on socio-economics, ideologies. All in the name of progress in a meaningless world.

The also German existentialist Martin Heidegger (1889 – 1976 A.D.) produced a new concept, that of *Dasein*, i.e. the concept of *being* that permeates and envelops our physical existence, but without resorting to any transcendental or theological roots. This *Dasein* was the purest form of existential meaning that could be derived from atheism, and appears to give continuation to Arthur Schopenhauer's (1788 – 1860 A.D.) "The World as Will" concept – a perpetual zeitgeist (spirit of the age) of sorts, or if preferred an invisible source for what motivates humans to act as they do. The main difference is Schopenhauer's *Will* was attributed to the world, while Heidegger's *Dasein* to the individual, but both present an intangible root for human agency that does not require any otherworldly phenomena. The latter can be seen as the authentic inner-self that is immersed in the everyday world but without being ensnared by it. A way of existing, being, but without the soul.

But others such Stuart Mill, Marx and Engels took a different approach, focusing mostly on socioeconomic models that follow up on Schopenhauer's *Will*, but in a more clinical, cold hearted manner, resulting in utilitarianist, socialist and communist rhetoric that still afflict contemporary societies. These ideologies and currents of thought, led to the growth of the atheist ethos, metastasizing across Western countries and around the world. This man-made solutions left the door wide open for the path of Post-modernism, most notably celebrated

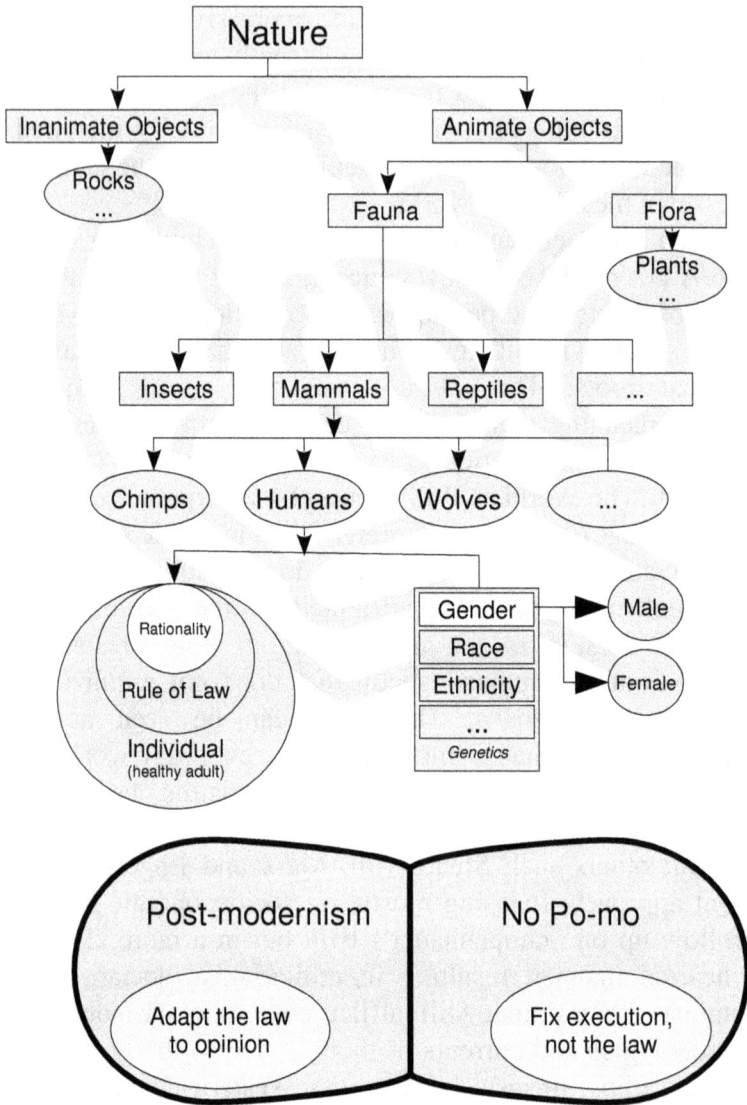

Figure 36: The irrationality of post-modernism

by the French philosopher   Jean-Paul Sartre (1905 – 1980 A.D.), and the path of Post-structuralism, with the fellow countrymen Jacques Derrida (1930 – 2004 A.D.) and Michel Foucault (1926 – 1984 A.D.) in the very front seats to begin deconstructing the "abstract ideas" that designed, and came from, the past. They formed the guild of the *friends of misery*, but where did the rise of these ideologies riddled with eugenics, dysgenics, abstractionism and relativism came to be?

With the ancient depicted as archaic, their obsolescence purportedly fruit of foolish religious views and antiquated methods and technologies, it became apparent the requirement to carve a new path. This process of deracination is a clear result of the post-industrial era, where the fancy for technological innovations became synonymous with progress. And still remains this way today – after all, who thinks a mobile phone version 8 is better than the model of the same brand version 12? Or a car that comes equipped with GPS and hybrid systems is worse than the one with none of this new technological gadgets and gimmicks? The fast pace at which scientific, technological and medical discoveries took place may have indelibly negative side effects in the human spirit.

The Christian principle of protecting the ones and the ideas of those who came before, was superseded by "Destroy the past, so you can progress into the future". Even nature fell victim to whimsical preference, with the absurdity of personal identity supposedly overriding biology through *gender identity*. Post-modernist and Post-structuralist societies will inevitably fall victim of fashionable and current trends, even the irrational ones. The law or principles swerve one way or the other based on the demands of the ones with the loudest opinions, instead of fixing the application (and execution) of sturdy laws that were shown to yield outstanding results. Christianity is replaced by the fouls gold, where a promise of Heaven on Earth seduces the simple minded who believe playing God is an eligible answer for humanity's success and happiness.

EXISTENTIALISM 2.0

a farmless ant-farm

During the Classical period in Europe, the Ancient Greek philosopher Plato (428 – 327 B.C.) developed the *Theory of Forms* in an effort to provide an explanation for how humans are capable of interpreting world phenomena and objects. The theory states there are immaterial essences that are absolute and immutable for everything we experience in the real world, which in turn are nothing more than objects onto which these *forms* project their singular qualities. As such, an object in the real world will be a *particular* that possesses many *universals*, i.e. multiple characteristics that are 'cast' onto it. For example, if a person sees a golden cat, they will identify it as a cat because there is a perfect, unchanging, timeless *form* of a cat that all humans were born with in their minds. This will include the fact that a cat is an animal that walks on four legs, is furry, has a tongue, two eyes, whiskers and meows; and in this case this *particular* cat also has the *universal* characteristic of being of a golden color. If the same person then sees a golden dog, a lot of the *universals* mentioned above will be shared with the cat but instead of meowing it will bark, making it possible to distinguish, along with many other *universals* that belong to the perfect *form* of dog but not the cat, between the two objects. In essence, *forms* allow the human mind to intelligibly differentiate different real-world tangible objects, *particulars*, to be grouped based on their shared *universals*. These concept where the *forms* appear perfect and predefined in a transcendental state is referred to as *Realism*.

In the Post-classical era, and throughout the centuries in Europe, this theory was highly contested or simply confusing, mainly due to the fact that some *forms* were perceived as subjective, such as *beauty*, and the idea that humans are born with 'built-in' perfect ideas does not explain how they are or where they come from. Some philosophers or scholars simply disliked the idea of these esoteric *forms* existing at all.

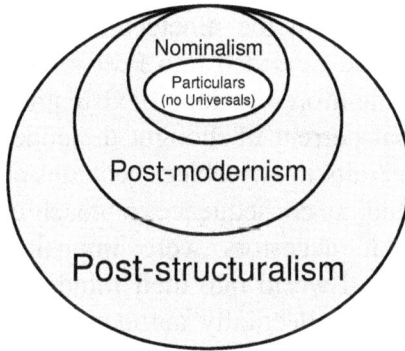

Figure 37: The roots of post-modernism

An Italian Dominican friar and philosopher, Thomas Aquinas (1225 – 1274 A.D.) came up with a solution he named *Moderate Realism* and the solution was quite simple and conferred validity to both *particulars* and *universals*: instead of being born with these perfect *forms* embedded in their minds, people acquired them through experience. That is, once witnessing a cat or a representation of it, such as a drawing, a person would acquire that specific *form*, carrying it in their mind until death. Unfortunately, around the same period in the fourteenth century, unsatisfied with Plato's idea, the English Franciscan friar William of Ockham (1287 – 1347 A.D.) came up with an alternative that he called *Nominalism* (**Figure 37**). This vised to get rid of the *universals* altogether by claiming these to be mere abstract, subjective attributes fashioned by humans to restrict the definition and identity of the material objects themselves. The *particulars* are thus still fully accepted as existent but in a unique, single form. The characteristics that are shared between each of the *particulars* (the *universals), are* are illusory and decreed as mere constructs of human will.

Much later on in the nineteenth century this concept was picked upon and extended into Post-modernism and Post-structuralism by the aforementioned existentialist philosophers and others. In that current of thought the concept of common characteristics or traits in any object becomes an imposition on human thought and, as consequence, a breach on their freedom of thinking. Their ancestors were imposing such archaic portrayals of the real world into their minds, thereby hindered their ability to be intellectually autonomous. A cat, a dog, a horse, a color, even beauty and good or evil, all are in the eye of the beholder. It wasn't too long until generations of youths became intellectually handicapped and injected with redefinitions to the degree that even gender and race, among others, are now subject to the individuals whimsical preference – they became so open-minded to the point their brains fell out. Their ability to freely identify as whatever they choose overrides any sense of objectivity and the *particular* becomes its own king – the *Dasein* as a universe within itself.

Subject to no law, and fed with hatred for their own predecessors and all their traditions and customs, a repulsion

for Christian doctrine and one of its Ten Commandments –
(Exodus 20:12) "Honor thy father and mother" – each
generation is deracinated from the previous in a perpetual
series of ritualistic murder-suicide degenerate jitters that serves
no purpose other than to allow the puppet masters, the ones that
want to rule them all, to pull strings in the midst of all chaos
and anarchy. This results in a ceremony that gives the deluded
herd full freedom to rush towards the cliff – a vision that would
make Nietzsche spin in his own grave, and it probably does.

Under Christianity, *new* isn't synonymous to *good*, as
there is more to morality than innovation. In fact, the spiritual
does not necessarily evolve alongside the material. Sometimes,
if not many, revolutions in technologies and science and serve
as an antigenic to the soul. The fine balance between these two
natures we are made of should not be tampered with. Atheism
(of the real kind) unavoidably will, as it conflates novelty with
happiness, with the blatant effects that can be widely seen
pervading the entirety of the globe in nefarious way in the
current period of the early twenty-first century.

PERMISSIVENESS OF ATHEISM

a lie is a lie, no matter how many tongues speak it

With the umbilical cord that connects humans to spirituality
severed and the ethos subordinate to the philosophy of atheism,
sentience becomes an illusion and the Nietzschean paradigm
"Nothing is forbidden, everything is permitted" is king. Under
such permissiveness cultist movements and ideologies such as
utilitarianism, faux-atheism, Marxism, socialism and neo-
Marxism strive. Soon the *Order and Progress* posit takes over

the Christian culture of love, worthiness, integrity, devotion and happiness, thus crippling the quest for metaphysical meaning. The meaninglessness of the being is all there is left.

The Christian paradigm known as *The Golden Rule*, straight from the Biblical text – (Matthew 7:12) "In everything, therefore, treat people the same way you want them to treat you, for this is the Law and the Prophets." – is grounded on the spiritual. This concept as a law is something that atheists procured to high-jack without success because they removed the object it was attached to. The faux-atheist can only *prescribe* this rule, not assert it, and even then they should always remit the Christian version. The prohibitive version, i.e. the same principle but in its defensive form that infers self-preservation, comprises a simple principle that can be found abundantly in the wild kingdom. The genuine atheist however can open his eyes and come to full realization of what the atheistic Golden Rule(s) should be:

- To the <u>weak</u>: do *not* treat others the way you fear being treated.
- To the <u>strong</u>: treat others the way it benefits you the most.

The original rule should then be applicable only to large contingents of people who lack strength individually, hence compensating for it with large numbers. Ideologies such as Marxism follow this logic which make use of *dysgenics*, which consists of the idea of the weak being privileged over the strong. Nietzsche referred to this as *Nihilism*, where the weak forming large bodies, the masses, and in a herd-like behavior aim to take control of society. According to the German philosopher, and many would agree with this logic, the predominance of *quantity* over *quality* will inevitably lead to social malady and sickness, with the resultant societal collapse taking place. The weak exist in greater numbers *because* they are inferior, as it is normal as per nature's design, and therefore encounter failure easier then excellence. Nietzsche himself promoted an ideology that encouraged the polar opposite, i.e. *eugenics*, where the strong are privileged over the weak based on their superiority and greater capability of survival and success – as per prescription of Mother Earth. Add to both a slice of *utilitarianism* – which in a nutshell is the acceptance of sacrificing the few for the greater good of the many – and the fog hazily covering the socialist movements and revolutions from the twentieth century (and beyond) starts dissipating.

If the socialist-Marxist maxim is that of pitching the oppressed against the oppressor by the use of dysgenics, consequently legitimizing the necessary bloodshed required to overthrow the existing rulers, as well as the powerful and the wealthy, the promoters of eugenics used Nietzsche and Heidegger to pave the road to national socialism and fascism: the Nazi party of Adolf Hitler (1889 – 1945 A.D.) and the PNF of Benito Mussolini (1883 – 1945 A.D.). The so called far-left socialist-Marxists manipulated the masses to acquire power in the name of broader equality, order and progress, whereas the others, the so called far-right fascists, entered the same manipulation strategies but this time under the guise of economy recovery, rebirth of the empire and in the name of national pride.

One of the key outcomes of making a clear distinction between these two currents of thought, instead of bundling them together like they should be, was honored by the known adage "History is written by the victors". After World War II, particularly in Europe and North America, a brainwashing propaganda machine spread out like wild fire and proceeded to indoctrinate Western nations into presenting the Nazis, or Hitler, with the *evil* epithet and the allies, Roosevelt, Churchill and Stalin, as *good*. Even throughout the Cold War the propagation of the black and white, good vs evil narrative never ceased making its way into movies, books, documentaries, mainstream media and education institutions. Instead of demonstrating what the Nazis did, every of their actions was classified as *evil*. Conversely, all the actions and conduct of the allies was justified, and therefore *good*. If anyone were to walk through the streets of any Western city with a cap on with a German Nazi Swastika on it, certainly they would be stopped or cussed that, but in equivalence, if someone were to wear a shirt with the Communist Party traditional symbol of the hammer and sickle, nothing with result from that.

The reality is we were told *what* to think, not *how* to think. At least when it comes to politics and ideology this is a fact, although in the current Western environment it's evident the cancerous growth of the problem. The objective observation is that Hitler wasn't evil because he killed Jews in concentration camps, but simply that he *killed*. Even the numbers of their Semite victims was inflated in order to sensationalize the event further, and hence devaluing and even jeering at the suffering of these people as if lower death numbers would have been of less significance. It's a known fact that Auschwitz, which harbored the largest facilities in terms of prisoner capacity and gas chambers, and the other couple of dozen or so camps, are unlikely to have led to the claimed six million people killed, and more likely two-thirds of those originally estimated numbers. But the figures presented are accurate or not, the deaths caused by the Nazi regime, which will probably remain forever enshrouded in doubt because a lot of the records were destroyed by them as the allies closed in, led to the blatantly obvious subsequent special treatment to the Jews that sought exile in other Western countries. As this occurred, quickly the label of "protected group" sprung. This was the stepping stone to the current tribal climate of privilege through victimhood, with the effects *feminism* distinctly brought to the West thrown in for good measure.

The post-war narrative has thence been prescriptive instead of informative, subverting the original Christian design of individual sovereignty and ensuant loss of agency from the populations of Western nations – no point in having freedom if you don't know how to use it, that is through a sound thinking process. The psychosomatic repulsion for the Nazi Swastika but the acceptance of any communist symbols is an unsubtle display of hypocrisy and ignorance, since the latter regimes killed well over ten times what the regime that started World War II did. Even to this day it's controversial to question the symbols and numbers mentioned here without the fear of being labeled a bigot, a racist or even a Nazi.

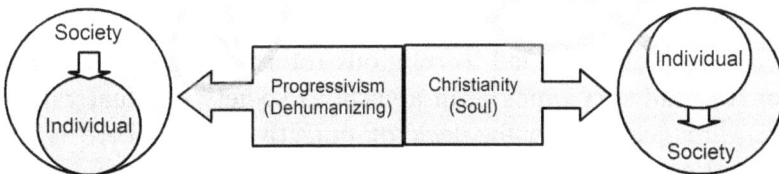

**Figure 38: Christianity from within,
atheism from without**

Christian Liberal Democracies were built from the individual outwards, i.e. the focus of society is on the individual, not the whole, as per **Figure 38**. Agency depends on knowledge provided by crystal-clear, untainted, unbiased information. Laws and rules are based on the value of the individual as a human being, not as a cog in the machine, a mere, insignificant part of a whole. Without this clutter-free mindset the muddled thought and the inability to accomplish an healthy thinking process (*how* to think), the herd mentality takes over, finding solace in exclusively what the elites and rulers feed them with. Favoritism and nepotism divide the social fabric and true *equality* and *equity* are not possible, as Christianity would have wanted them. There are no equal opportunities and no fairness in judgment, instead everything is biased and corrupted. Through the means of victimhood and pity, a sort of *charitable equity* – a *sameness* – is pursued under the guise of protecting the weaker, persecuted groups. Everyone is identical, just like units in the system.

STOICISM OF RELIGION

unto God what is Caesar's

The rise of atheism led to religious reform taking place, only for it to fail very quickly. In a vacuous society spiritual values are shredded due to the lack of objectivity – if there is no natural origin to these values other than opinion, emotion and preference then the social landscape is refactored under such paradigm. In the West the Bible furnished societies with ethical norms and spiritual principles, which is, as it should, the end purpose of religion, not science, economics or history. This represents part of secularism but under atheism everything breaks apart because there is no Church nor Scriptures, resulting in a void being created – one that transcends the competence of a belief system that does not look outside the realm of the material.

Atheists are proficient in victimizing themselves, claiming persecution by religious people, using the emotional model of "He who cries the loudest gets the most attention", when in fact they are the ones of misbehave, deride and criticize who opposes or disagrees with them. Indeed without the spirit a human's journey is left under the control of the body, which in turn is under the command of emotions and personal views or group preferences. If Jewish people were the first post-war privileged group ingratiated with this newly found strategy, the main aspect to read from the subsequent consequences is that victimization or pity create a multi-tiered society. Today we witness a chain of oppression built and climbed by the weakest, most unsuccessful and incompetent individuals in the incessant acquisition of advantages and benefits in detriment of the ones who do all the hard work, in a wretched demonstration of spiritual hunger. Organized chaos, replete of degeneracy, infantility, dysfunction and animality prevails. Sodom and Gomorrah all over again.

Atheism doesn't work, so why redesign societal models in the name of improvement since Christianity does? Walk a mile on His shoes – suffering, humiliation, persecution, the true pursuit of science and knowledge from His followers such as Da Vinci, Newton, Galileo, Descartes, Kepler, etc. the list is endless. Before this intrusive, endemic belief system started corrupting the West, Christian doctrine taught us to accept the past and honor our ancestors and to live in the present to build the future. There were no *progressivist* fables or magic formulas offering unattainable idyllic societies; no change for the sake of change; a fake meaning in a meaningless universe; no emotion over reason or body over mind.

Christian values are objectively *better* due to historical results. Nations ruled under such principles have been at the front-end of human civilization for millennia. The ethical naturalistic rhetoric of the *collective conscious* cannot stand against the scrutiny of fact-value distinctions, which make a clear separation between axiomatic truths (prescriptive values based on opinion or preference, known as *value-terms*) and scientific statements (assertions made while supported by cognitive experiences), thence one can conclude the atheistic quest for progress is untenable. The reductivist failed arguments, like the idea that most societies carrying the Biblical "Thou shalt not kill" achieved it through a natural process of social human interactions, expose the lack of awareness that it's the details that are important. Christianity is an amazing success due to its wholesomeness, its fullness in providing spiritual guidance, unlike the Aztecs with Tezcatlipoca, Islam with Mohamed and Ancient Greece with Zeus and his Olympian entourage.

CHAPTER 8

Atheism is Not Great

SOCIALISM

the young – give them power and they won't know what do do

During the post-enlightenment era, at the end of the Industrial Revolution in nineteenth century Europe, the rise of socialism took place strengthened by the publishing of the works of Karl Marx (1818 – 1883 A.D.), advancing anti-capitalistic views and advocacy for worker and state ownership of the means of production. In 1864 the International Working Men's Association was established, commonly know as the *First International* due to the various successors that were founded decades later, with the intent to organize and unify the labor force in the European continent. It quickly was taken over by socialists and their multitude of schools of thought, out which Marxism was the more prevalent one. However, most can be classified as being subjacent to the ideologies of *anarcho-socialism* (usually known as *anarcho-communism*) and *state-socialism*.

Any type of socialist rhetoric is specious by nature due to its atheistic origins, promising heaven on Earth to compensate the fact they lack one in the after life, but inescapably ending up in hell. The anarchic theory is the most captivating to the socialist revolutionaries as its intention is to defer power from the government to the hands of the people, who will engage in self-management of common ownership of resources and all means of production. As it stands, the anarcho-communist *modus-operandi* is that of relieving the working class of any hierarchical structures of power. The model can then promote the slogan "To each according to his *contribution*", allowing for the model to be founded on anarchy. The anarchic model in turn requires a society without a ruler, thereby justifying the its prefix. However this strategy is doomed to fail as it's based on micro-management. Out of different models, the one where communes (a self-organized rural/industrial community) would be self-regulated appears to be the one that is feasibly theorized about, but this leaves a gap in how to macro-manage their interaction. Even if a particular commune were to exist in harmony and peaceful cooperation, there is little chance it would be self-sufficient, leading to high potential of problems when interacting with other communities. Another side-effect is that it could lead to hyper-specialization of certain communes that have a wide abundance of natural resources of a particular kind that is rare to find elsewhere, with the results of such ownership being detrimental to others who intend to acquire them through trade – indeed this would confer to this anarchic society a strong scent of capitalism. One could say that such model using communes could be replaced by general ownership of any means of production, but chaos would ensue. Anyone would be able take anything at any given time? What about disagreement, which is inbuilt in human nature and therefore unavoidable?

    Realistically this anarchic model relies primarily on the

laborer's *will* to produce instead of his *need*. Without a master regulatory entity such as a state or an aggregation of syndicates, the labor force would have to rely on a self-imposed discipline and mutual respect. At any given conflict or dissension, chaos would take over, since it would be next to impossible to endlessly agree on the *value* of what each laborer produces. Whether be it goods or services, they would persistently compare one-another when it comes to the value of their hard work. Adding to this array of problems the inalienable need to keep the laborer's *want* alive even after he attained the comforts of life he had set himself to achieve. This is because a successful, fulfilled worker would no longer have any need to do any work, thereby rendering defunct any ties with social collaboration. If a farmer is to have earned all he dreamed of, he could now hang his boots and choose not to be productive any longer, which doesn't seem like much of a problem – at least until instead of just one thousands leave the workforce. Some sort of common *will* would have to be present to counter the laborer's personal predisposition to retire early.

Invariably, any socialist revolution turns to state-socialism, where a centralized authority controls the means of production in the name of the people under the slogan "To each according to his *needs*". In these nanny-states all private property is made *public*, that is to say state owned as it's taken from private owner through a nationalization process. It is then put under government command, leaving the laborer completely subordinate to it. The most familiar examples are those of communist states functioning under Marxism-Leninism such as the Soviet Union, China, Vietnam, Cuba, etc. With the state in control of the economy it's imperative it also controls everything else: from the military to the police and, without exception, the secret services. Only then can such glorious quest in the name of the people can be put into practice, effectively turning a nation into a machine – a whole whose constituents merely form the parts of. Another symptomatic property of such regimes is autocracy, since if they took the power away from the people, why shouldn't they take the power away from the members of the party, even if only to a certain degree?

If one were to bring up a simple example of an island with one thousand inhabitants, out of which one percent own ninety percent of the wealth, this would pretty much sum up the *raison d'etre* for the existence of socialism. If the *many* were to revolt against the *few* that exploit them, by taking their lives or simply putting them on a boat and kicking them out, all the wealth of the island could now belong to the ones that successfully perpetrated the socialist coup.

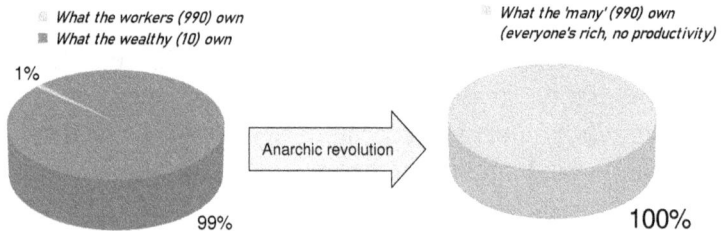

Figure 39: The island metaphor for anarcho-socialism

Under the anarcho-socialist model, the remaining inhabitants could now redistribute all the wealth among themselves, with each of them becoming instantly rich (**Figure 39**). No-one is left to do any of the work, as they all have an abundance of capital in the bank. But if the plumber needs food, he can ask the farmer for some eggs, who in turn will charge an exorbitant amount of money, as they both have it in plenty but little need for it. Reciprocally, if the farmer wants to have his drain pipes fixed, or needs to take a cab somewhere, or his tractor needs parts for repair, everything will be extremely expensive. That is because money is an illusion, fit only as a *representation* of labor. Real capital is human capital, that is human effort and hard-work utilized to produce goods and provide services. This shows the gullibility – if not sheer stupidity – of the ones that advocate for socialism of the anarchic kind.

One could still keep the anarchic model, but this time ridding the islanders of money altogether. With everyone free of that curse, what would motivate the farmer to wake up at five in the morning to milk the cow and feed the chicken? Others would come over and take the product of his hard work for nothing. Without going down the socialist rabbit hole of *labor theories of* value, one could claim there would be a mutual agreement between all the inhabitants of the island. But who would draft it? Even worse, who would be in charge of enforcing it? Once the dust settles it becomes clear without anyone in command it's a free for all. Anarchy is completely dependent on goodwill and agreement, making this model solely suitable for angelical entities, certainly not highly flawed creatures like human beings. Needless to say, in the four Internationals (the worker federations that debated socialism as a means to unify the labor force up until the mid-twentieth century) never managed to come to a full agreement on how to implement such ideology.

Turning to state-socialism (**Figure 40**), the obvious answer within this scenario of the island inhabitants is much easier to understand. With the abundance of socialist implementations of this kind, it's easy to deduce that, after the islanders rid themselves of the ten percent that were exploiting them, a small group of individuals would prosecute a power grab, thereby quickly and effectively replacing the previous exploiters, only to emerge as the new ones – but this time all the name of public health, equality and happiness. In Russia the czars were killed, only for communist despots to take their place and kill over twenty-five million by starvation and gulags. Identically, in China the emperor was deposed, so the ones claiming to care about the workers could kill over forty million people in the pursuit of their socialist ideal. In reality it was never about the peoples, not the ones at the bottom at least. Socialist states have no need for money as they have direct access to what truly matters – power over others.

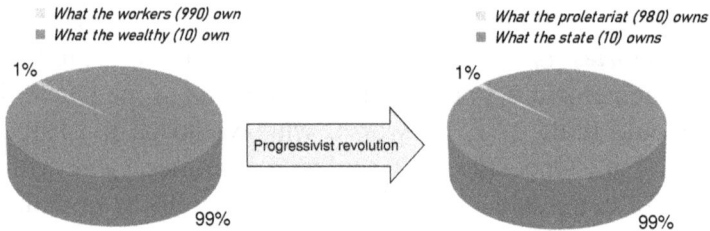

Figure 40: The island metaphor for state-socialism

THE MARXIST FAR-LEFT

to pitch the oppressed against the oppressor

Where with socialism the debate is *who* controls the means of production, with communism the emphasis is put on *how* to make such means common to all. In both cases the maxim "To abolish private property" was utilized in their crusade against the evils of capitalism – that is in fact the socialist maxim. Enter the German philosopher and economist Karl-Marx (1818 – 1883 A.D.), who's doctrine was founded on the arrogation of any power and wealth from the wealthy bourgeoisie only to then place them in the hands of the proletariat. His three-volume compendium *Das Kapital,* the full of which was posthumously published with strong collaboration from his lifelong friend Friedrich Engel (1820 – 1895 A.D.), was nothing short of an anti-capitalist rant, with little to offer beyond the highly destructive revolutionary act that proclaimed to dismantle the unjust and unfair capitalist societal model that favored the rich. This revolution, no matter how much bloodshed or heads severed, is envisaged in a retaliatory fashion, so the oppressed can destroy their oppressors. In complete contrast with the Christian principle of non-retaliation of turning the other cheek – (Mathew 5:39) "Whoever slaps you on your right cheek, turn the other to him also" – the Marxist principle of retaliation provides an immunity shield to the masses that march inexorably towards fratricide, their victims becoming the new oppressed.

Marxist dialectic is fully focused on achieving a materialistic socioeconomic equilibrium upon the defeat of 'functional contradictions' of the societal model. Based on this doublespeak, the oppressed are actually actively engaging in oppression as they undertake the effort to reach such goal. Were it not for this biased, hypocritical, and one could say supremacist exemption status, they would have to then confer themselves as the new oppressor and their target (the previous 'oppressor') as the new oppressed, entering a never-ending and autophagic back-and-forth cycle until none remained. All out of pure aggression and self-righteousness (**Figure 41**).

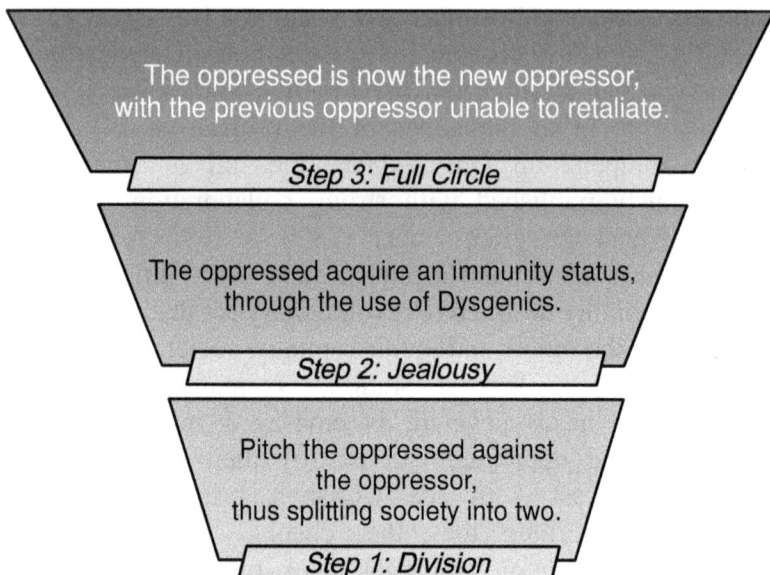

Figure 41: The three steps of Marxism indoctrination

When guided by Marxist philosophy, if a neighbor throws a brick through one's window, he then throws *two* bricks through his neighbor's. In fact plenty are the advocates of that rotten ideology that preemptively declare to be in danger from such neighbor – maybe they observed a glint in his eye as he watered his front yard, or perhaps he were a shirt with a saying to their dislike. This stratagem permits the Marxist to make the first strike as a "preventive" measure. With Christianity, in the event of having a brick thrown through the window as before, one would call the police and defer to the authorities and courts any restraining orders, or other forms of punishment, and to the insurance companies the sum to be paid by the neighbor for the respective damages – but only *after* the occurrence took place in the real world, not in the supposed victim of oppression's mind as a figment of their imagination.

Under the guise of having the moral high ground, Marxists will release themselves from the burden of oppression by any means necessary. However first rules must be brought about to define the category of *oppressed*: who to protect and who to save? Classical-Marxism (known as Marxism-Leninism) pitches the poor against the rich and the workers against the proprietors. The more recent neo-Marxism (also known as cultural-Marxism) wages a cultural war, tossing races, sexualities and genders against each other. For example, *equality* is one of the main victims of either type of Marxism, where equal opportunities used to take place under egalitarianism by not hindering anyone from their quest for personal achievement. This was done regardless of superficial traits and instead focusing on merits resulting in true equity, i.e. fairness and justice. Under Marxism discrimination in pursuit of sameness became rampant, as everything is based on skin-deep grounds in order to appease the epileptic mob. An unmistakable indicator of this is *affirmative action* that reigns supreme in the current Western societies in order to deliver the neo-Marxist favorites *diversity* and *inclusion*, instead of allowing individual worthiness and skill to do the job.

In conclusion, Marxism is a supremacist ideology based on moral superiority that can be split into a three-step system: firstly comes *division*, where society breaks into two groups labelled the oppressed and oppressor; secondly comes *jealousy*, as the oppressed acquire an immunity status by virtue of *dysgenics*, where the weak annihilate the strong, the ugly deface the beautiful, the cowardly take down the brave, the poor steal from the rich, the obtuse deprive the intelligent, the unproductive leech off the productive, the failed ruin the successful; finally and thirdly comes the *full circle*, where the ones calling themselves oppressed have now become the oppressors, but will not give up their seats in positions of power out of their delusion of superiority – that is how supremacy works after all.

A prime illustration of how the Marxist ideology is carried out in a real world scenario is the Cuban revolution. Initially Che Guevara (1928 – 1967 A.D.) and his peers guided the country towards a socialist utopia chanting the catchphrase "Viva la revolución", with all the fable-like ingredients and bells and whistles typical of this ideology being used to mobilize the crowds and the revolutionaries. After the bloodshed, once the donkeys chasing the plastic carrot – looking so yummy, shiny and delicious – suddenly hit their heads against the wall and gain awareness (with a severe headache thrown into the mixture) that the whole thing was imaginary. Lastly, it's time for the cynics to move in, as was the case with Fidel Castro (1926 – 2016 A.D.) and his entourage, to rip the benefits of the reality of socialism. The utopia has now come to full realization and everyone is finally equal – equally miserable that is, as poverty and repression abound.

THE FASCIST FAR-RIGHT

to become the imperialistic oppressor

The term Fascism comes from a tool (from Latin called *fasces)* that was used as a symbol of official authority the magistrates possessed in the ancient Roman empire. It was adopted by Benito Mussolini (1883 – 1945 A.D.) reflecting the strict rule and leadership of the party he led, the National Fascist Party (PNF for the Italian acronym). Even though the adopted movement of *nationalism* was an inherent part of the fascistic ideology, the focus on state-socialism took precedence over everything else, in that his government would control any access to the means of production while allowing land and industrial ownership. The regimes that took over in Spain under Francisco Franco (1892 – 1975 A.D.) and Portugal under António de Oliveira Salazar (1889 – 1970 A.D.) had the same fascistic tinge, all operating within economies that can be classified as corporativist dictatorships. As a matter of fact it's possibly to bring a quote from the early twentieth century fascistic dictator of Italy, Mussolini himself: "Fascism should more properly be called corporatism because it is the merger of state and corporate power".

Corporations were thence nothing more than politico-economical instruments as they found themselves subject to strict political control of the fascistic government. Traditional socialists will object to the comparison due to the roots of these ultra-nationalist regimes being proponents of an exacerbated sense of pride, and even perhaps superiority, when it comes to their cultural, ethnic, religious and other ancestral unifying distinctions, but it stands to reason that despite some dissimilarities, the heavily totalitarian, militaristic and dictatorial political systems fall very tightly within state-socialist framework – indeed they have a lot more in common then otherwise. In Germany, the National Socialist German Workers' Party, with the byname of Nazi Party, commanded by Adolf Hitler (1889 – 1945 A.D.) was no different other than the

the championing of the superiority of the Aryan race, involving a white supremacist view of the world, but otherwise achieving the same results. Where Nazi Germany had the Gestapo, the USSR had the KGB; where the first had concentration camps controlled by the SS, the second had labor death camps controlled by the Gulag. All other such regimes had equivalent agencies to deal with dissidents to the cause.

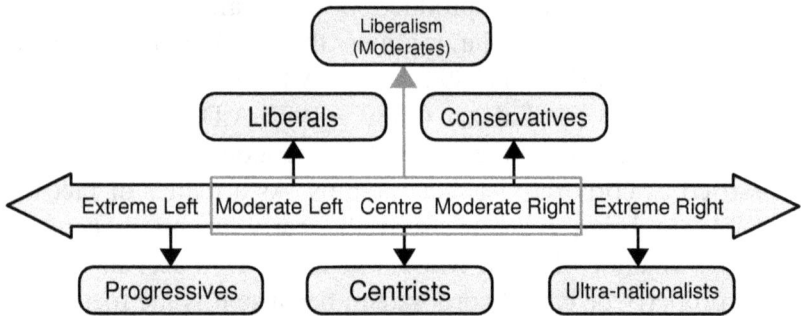

Figure 42: The range of the political spectrum

If Liberalism forms the mid-range of the political spectrum, both extremes will share fascism in its general form in the sense of displaying complete intolerance towards any opposition. Whether those authoritarian views are progressive, reactionary or nationalist is irrelevant, as it's the authoritative element that poses a threat to anyone with the 'wrong' opinion. The focus should therefore be put on the *extreme* (or *far)* part of the definition, not what particular recipe is attached to it.

Herein lies the truth of the socialist ideology: for the peoples to be tended to, a nanny-state must to be instated. That state requires power, which in turn leads to a totalitarian octopus that inserts itself into every corner and crevice of the society it was instructed to rule over. Intolerance, suppression and persecution are paramount, irrespective of reactionary tendencies or not. Unlike with Christianity with its *principle of presumption of innocence*, where tangible evidence is necessary to be brought forward by the accuser so a sentence must be carried out, these profoundly atheistic models – whether by cause or action, if they dare claim to be otherwise – enforce a system based on the *principle of presumption of guilt*, where the accuser's word is, by virtue of his own superiority, enough to sentence. As per **Figure 43**, power lies in a series of concentric circles of power, with the inner layers cannibalizing any 'suppressive' individuals lying in the outer layers, with anyone lying outside the circles of power having no word or say altogether.

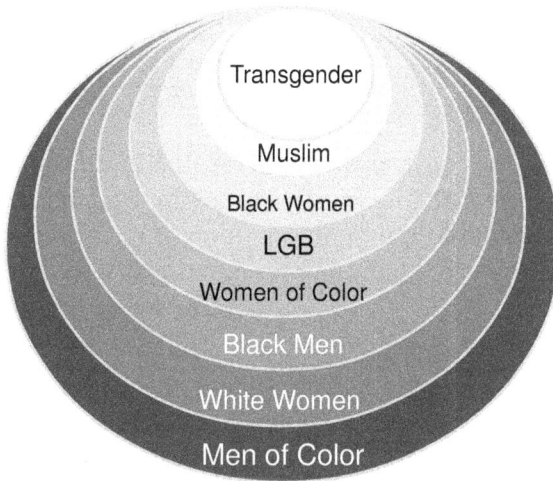

Figure 43: Woke-socialism chain of oppression

This effect can be visibly witnessed in a figurative the contemporaneous West, with the *woke* (neo-Marxist) chain of oppression designed to attribute positions of advantage from a cultural perspective. They scream like spoiled children to get attention and make the most outrageous demands based on their levels of victimhood, ending up in what is colloquially, and scornfully, referred to as the *Oppression Olympics*. This topic however will not be addressed here but further explored in a following chapter. Regardless of the condiments, supremacy is the key ingredient to explain the cannibalistic practices. If not for the superiority factor (based on whatever criteria dependent on each regime) offered to the factions as they approach the inner core, such presumption of guilt, and the blind authority that comes with it, would not be possible.

THE TRUE MODEL

three axis, not one

The traditional political model presented to all constituents for electoral voting acts is invariably a single-dimensional model that relies on the *left*, in representation of the workers and labor force, and the *right*, commonly associated with the corporate, industrial and property owners. These are directly related to the original seating arrangement in the parliament of France formed right after the end of the French revolution in 1789, known officially as the French National Assembly, where the bourgeoisie, high clergy and nobility seated to the right and the low clergy, low bourgeoisie and commoners to the left. However this definition leaves a lot to be desired since there are further motivations within the world of politics when choosing which side to take and how far along that side to go. Because of this, a great deal of confusion often erupts when trying to establish one's own position in the modern political spectrum.

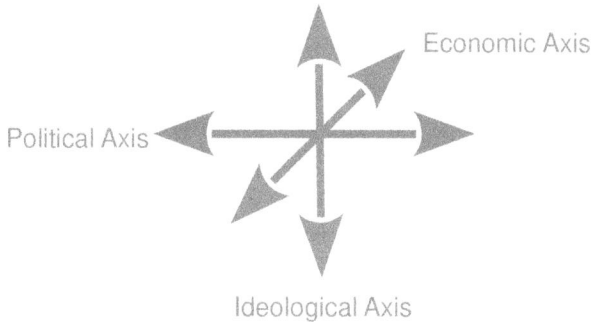

Figure 44: The three-axis political model

The reality is there are *three* main axis when it comes to each constituent's leanings: the *Ideological*, the *Political* and the *Economic*, as seen in **Figure 44**. Different political parties, or an individual's opinion, can frequently match each others views on one axis and discord on another. Starting with the *ideological* axis, the spectrum can be characterized as progressive on the far-left, shifting all the way into ultra-nationalism on the far-right. On the *political* axis, totalitarianism is at the left-end of the spectrum, with libertarianism at the opposite extreme. Finally, the *economic* axis ranges from socialist views on the left towards capitalistic ones on the right. The first and third axis allow for moderate perspectives in the mid-range, usually referred to as moderates or liberalism. Some muddiness can arise from the fact that moderate-leftists are often literally called *liberal*, while moderate-rightists called *conservative*. There is no other available term for moderate-left proponents, but liberalism comes from the idea of personal freedoms, individual rights, equality, democracy and having an open mind to exchange ideas, which all moderates must possess, otherwise such nomenclature wouldn't suit them. Conservatives may protect the *known* in the name of honoring their ancestry but are open to change, even if in a more restricted manner.

Within the *Ideological Spectrum* (**Figure 45**), progressivism can be outlined as the political doctrine of reform to achieve progress over individual interests, with the more radicals often promoting rushing into the unknown – change for the sake of change – all in the name of an utopian society. The socialist progressivist ideology of Marxism is the unequivocal favorite and therefore the socialist ideology most regularly chosen for the left to lead progressive movements. In an attempt at deconstructing well established power structures, for then to redesign society under a new paradigm, they start with a revolution and end with something (supposedly) modern, free of all ties with what these movements see as archaic and obsolete. Only by destroying the past they believe they can have a positive, fresh, new start. In stark contrast, ultra-nationalists tend to have an extreme, often supremacist, position on their culture, ethnicity and ancestry, and can be seen as an ideology with imperialistic and reactionary inclinations, with each nation operating with a great deal of disregard towards other nations. Ultra-conservatism has no such preference in favoring the nation over the individual but instead it's a political doctrine of fiercely protecting the things the ones who adopt it are familiar with, holding on to their culture, ancestry and cultural values.

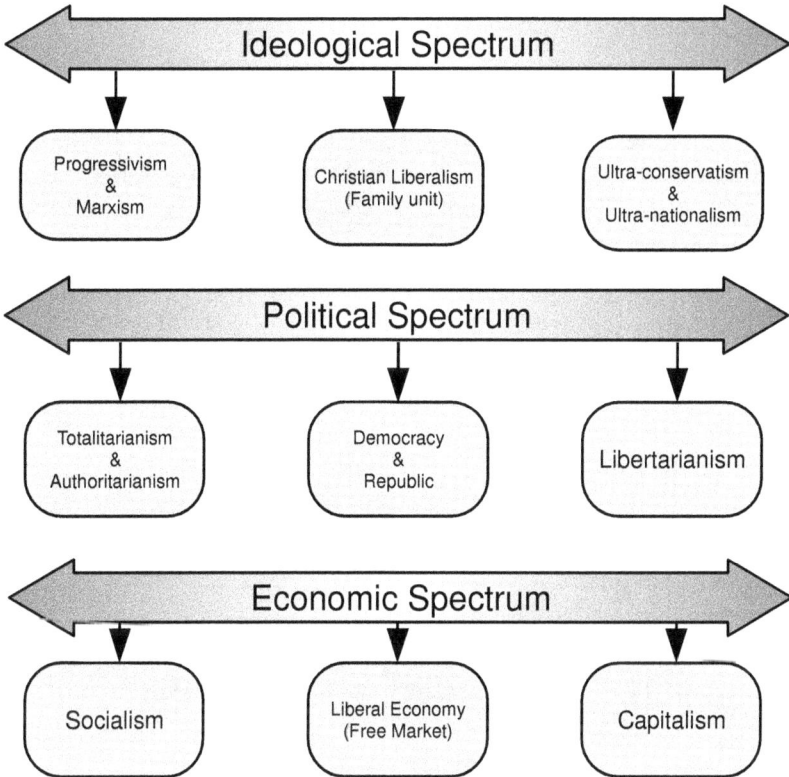

Figure 45: The three spectra

Within the *Political Spectrum*, which is more rigid by nature and there's strong limitation in terms of going either *left* or *right*, totalitarianism is the political system of ruling through stern authority within an ideology, spreading its tentacles to enforce it. Authoritarianism is not too dissimilar but this political system bases its rule through authority outside the grasp of any specific ideology. At the other end of the scale, libertarianism procures the least government interference possible in relation to the individual – some wishing no government at all. Democracy is the happy-medium, allowing governments to be elected by the people within certain time frames, while permitting individual rights and freedoms.

Within the *Economic Spectrum*, socialism is the model used where the state has full control over a country's economy, whether it has corporativist layers within it or not, and capitalism is the alternative that puts the focus on private entrepreneurship, initiative and ownership. In the middle of the spectrum, there are the liberal (or free market) economies, which often get mistaken by capitalism – or even socialism when convenient. The truth is liberal economies are formed by compounding socialism (state control) and capitalism (private ownership), allowing both to co-exist in a somewhat harmonious manner.

IDEOLOGICAL EXTREMISM

the bigger the promise, the greater the lie

Extremist movements, political parties or ideologies often depend on Populism, which is a political stance where anti-establishment demagogy is used as a mean to an end. The sales pitch can differ but the results are inescapably identical: the more rotten they are, the more they promise. If the fascist party of Mussolini promised an illustriously proud nation, a resurgence of the Roman empire, if only in a romanticized fashion, it ended up an autocracy where forcible suppression of any opposition took place, subordinate to the arbitrary will of a despotic ruler. Comparing it to the communist party of Stalin, it's hard to spot the difference, as both required a big government and an almighty state with full authority over the nation they rule. Whether the system of government is ultra-nationalistic or progressivist makes little to no difference when it comes to the extreme use, and abuse, of authority. An objection could be made by progressives when moving towards *globalism*, where the nation state disappears and a globalized economy would take over. However under the loss of the people's autonomy to choose their leaders a dictatorship, or a multitude of them, would emerge out of necessity. The obvious conclusion is that either progressive or ultra-conservative, extreme ideologies are required to be the far-left when it comes to the *political spectrum* (**Figure 46**).

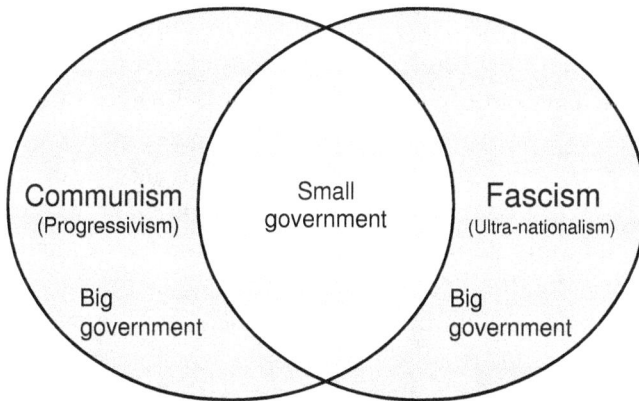

Figure 46: The nature of Extremism

Looking at the fascist movements that preceded World War II

(Hitler/Mussolini/Salazar/Franco), we can assert them to be ideologically extreme-right but politically and economically far-left, displaying ultra-nationalist, reactionary (in the sense of wishing for the rebirth of a long gone idealized era or empire), totalitarian and state-socialist dispositions accordingly. The Communists of the Soviet Union on the other hand, under Joseph Stalin (1878 – 1953 A.D.) and China under Mao Zedong (1893 – 1976 A.D.), along with a whole plethora of other communist regimes that are too many to enumerate, can be clearly identified as being ideologically, politically and economically far-left – they followed Marxist, totalitarian and state-socialist dispositions respectively.

There is also the recent socialist-corporativist model implemented in modern China, where a pseudo-capitalistic layer is placed on top of what otherwise can be perceived as a communist reality. China under the CCP went from a Buddhist country, where the beauty of the zen culture and spiritual principles were embedded into a classical Eastern society, to the Marxist ant-colony model of Mao, failing as much as any other classical communist model. Currently in their present model pseudo-freedoms and pseudo-private-ownership can instantly be revoked by the ruling tyrannical party, rendering its citizens nothing more than consumerist-ants, producing and consuming for the sake of the regime's machine lubrication. This Chinese model is nearly identical to the Nazi/Fascist model of the far-right dictatorships, where corporations do exist but under strict government control, under the penalty of closure, or even imprisonment of its owners. Through such a thin veil of deception it's fairly easy to observe, with eyes wide open and a mind as so, that these 'capitalist' models are nothing more than state-socialist nations just like any other that existed previously.

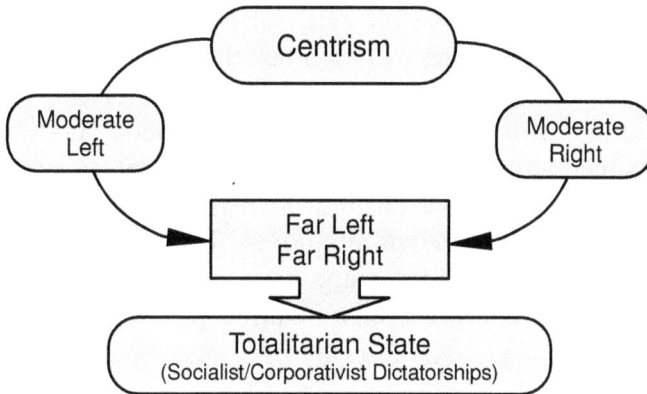

Figure 47: The true political spectrum

To accurately understand the reason for these similarities put into question, the *political spectrum* must be depicted in a different fashion: instead of using a linear left-to-right range, one should instead perceive centrism as the starting point at the top of a circle (or ellipse in the case of **Figure 47**), then move in a circular fashion from both the left and the right until finally both points meet, resulting in a socialist dictatorship. In this case the *economic spectrum* would necessarily be tied to this change, since despotic regimes cannot operate under genuine private ownership, thus making a state-socialist economy (corporativist or not) obligatory. The fact that economies we usually refer to as capitalist are actually free market economies comes from the problem of full private-ownership. True capitalism has never been tried because it would require the removal of all types of government and, consequentially, any state owned and controlled infra-structures and resources, such as roads, energy, the police and even the military. All these would subsequently be created, subsidized and managed by corporations, individuals or families that would own not only the land where its employees would live but instate laws and regulations within a delimited territory. Such model is not impossible to implement, but highly unpractical, as losing a job or getting a new one would involve moving outside the perimeter of the previous employer. Thus far only science-fiction movies and video game have played around with this idea, albeit it never actually being implemented in the real world.

IDEOLOGICAL MODERATION

work hard, play hard

Through the middle of each spectrum, the moderate political doctrines of Liberalism, Centrism and Conservatism share common ground, permitting the interchange of ideas or strategies, which are self-explanatory in the *ideological spectrum*. In the *economic spectrum*, liberals advance more governmental power, that is to say more socialism, while attempting to remove power from the hands of the wealthy. Their justification is that with more wealth and resources channeled to the state can become a better provider for the people, at least in theory since they don't bring into the equation the incompetence and corruption that often ensue. Conservatism focuses on private ownership, delegating wealth and power to the people, thence the inclination towards capitalism. Centrists (including the center-left and center-right), require a more open-minded approach, sitting on the fence and giving predilection to whatever plans of action they may consider useful at the time. Irrespective of where one lies on the moderate range of the spectrum, in any of the three axis, it's imperative to allow for a certain inter-mixture of ideas and measures out of having to keep an open mind, conforming to the idea of being *liberal* (in its true form) in first place.

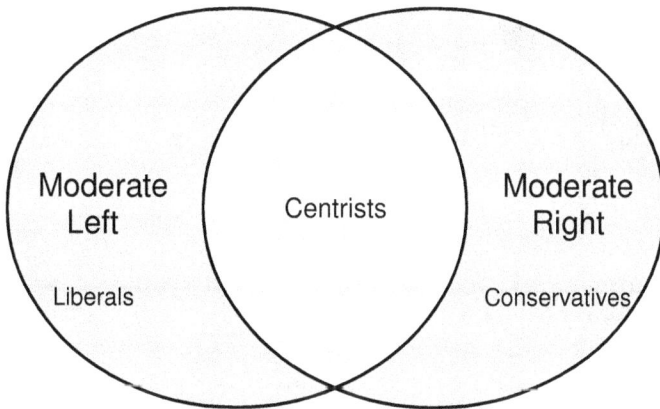

Figure 48: Moderation

A distinction between nationalism and ultra-nationalism has to be brought up. The former lies within the moderate range of the *Ideological Spectrum* and it refers to the idea of placing the nation in front of individual interests in a tolerant, patriotic, protective manner, but without the radicalisms involving supremacist views and alike. White-nationalism, for example, is a made up term to attempt to demonize nationalists from Europe and other Western countries, but nationalism cannot relate to race because there could be national interests in any given country that would conflict with racial or ethnic groups that live across borders. Taking the example of Denmark and Sweden, even though both countries are Scandinavian and share many similarities, suggesting that Danish nationalists would be perfectly happy if one million Swedes were to move there – and taking into consideration their current population is at just under six million and therefore would count as an appreciable intake – would be absurd, and vice-versa. The simple fact that both belong to the same ethnic and haplo group cannot be presented as substantive. Nationalism should thence be perceived as the ideology of patriotism to the point of sacrificing one's self for the nation, including protecting it from external interference or cultural pollution at all costs, and not something that can relate in any way to race or other internationally shared traits, even though some countries might have intrinsic and unique properties that would lead one to, erroneously, assume so.

CHAPTER 9

The Matriarchal Shift

THE POISONED APPLE OF MARXISM

one apple isn't enough

Feminism is a byproduct of Marxism, its poisoned apple in fact, offered to the recurrent victim of such seductive relish: the human female. Atheism carved the path to a vacuous social ethos, allowing attitudes and beliefs to be put into question under post-modernism and all ancestral practices and customs to be thrown out under post-structuralism. The original formula of the Marxist ideology – that of pitching the proletariat against the bourgeoisie – could then be reformulated in a cultural way, this time under the guise of women's rights, i.e. pitching women against men. The typical tribalism that originates from such nefarious ideology ensued and women used their predominant character trait, emotion that is, to pursue reforms that would result in the betterment of their condition – or so they claimed. This culture of emotivism later extended into other cultural realms related to race, ethnicity, parenthood, weight, etc. all subordinate to the idea of fighting bigotry having neo-Marxism as the end result.

In effect these claims of fighting preconceptions and social injustice result in the opposite, since it's feminism that offers a distorted lens of reality, which in turn is the very definition of prejudice. By viewing everything under the twisted perspective of such poisonous ideology society ends up adopting those problems, not getting itself rid of them – they instead keep piling up. Using rationality to observe reality and address social problems is the only way to prevent bigotry, without any recourse to the favoritism provided by emotions such as pity, victimhood, jealousy, retribution and so forth.

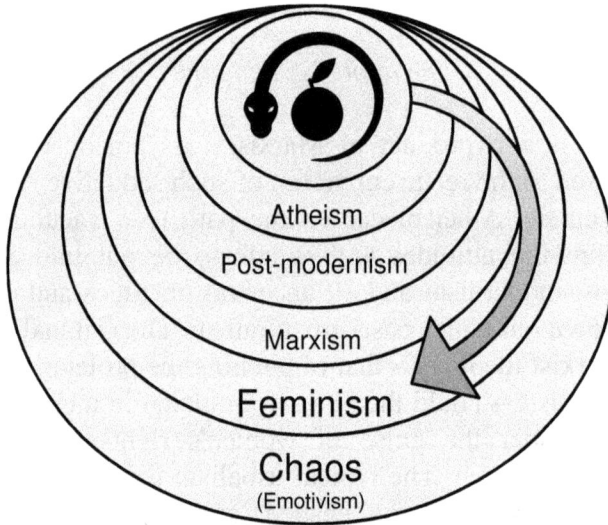

Figure 49: The poisoned apple of Marxism

Unfortunately what the female mind lacks in reason it makes up with emotion, which is an indelible and essential element in the familial context where there is an emotional bond to be nurtured and maintained, but leaves a lot to be desired when in the much wider social context where unfamiliarity abounds and closeness is scarce. The truth is one cannot be sexist, racist or take part in any other kind of prejudice by pointing out facts, seeing reality itself cannot be bigoted. This turns out to be a concept heavily foreign to the female mind, which procures a plain solution for social troubles by attempting to protect weaker groups, the ones that can be clearly identified by simplistic tribal traits. This is done in order to seek caring for the weak and vulnerable, in a obvious parallel to the power women themselves exerted over children for the entirety of our species existence.

Further to this, feminism was never designed to aid women but instead humiliate them. The paradigm of Marxism is that of a prosperous societal model based solely on socio-economics, completely disregarding the family, ancestral practices and religious values, leading to the reinforcement that only what men did, and still do, can be measured in terms of worth. The role fulfilled by women throughout human history is therefore thrown-out and made void. The first step consummated, that of humiliating women for their feminine traits, the participants in the movement will be sure to vacate their roles as mothers, lovers, home-makers and care-givers. The second step can now be taken (**Figure 50**) by filling in the emptiness by selling the conversion to masculinity, which more often than not makes the adherents delusional, as they tend to truly believe they can undertake such mission with success at lightning speed. The latter stage is achieved by joining the work force and becoming part of the socioeconomic machine, sickle in hand, sleeves up, jeans and headband, with little to no femininity left. The goal of feminism is thus achieved and women now take on a *competing* role, leaving behind the traditional *complementary* role that allowed humanity to evolve and reach the present civilizational level.

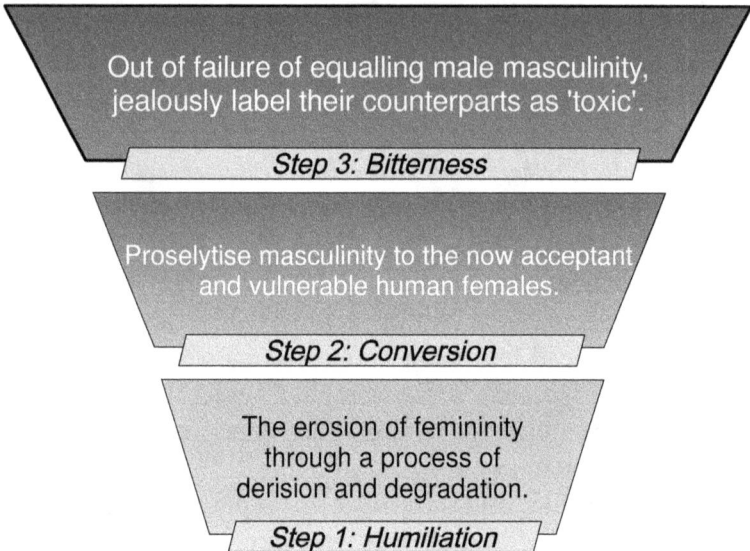

Out of failure of equalling male masculinity, jealously label their counterparts as 'toxic'.

Step 3: Bitterness

Proselytise masculinity to the now acceptant and vulnerable human females.

Step 2: Conversion

The erosion of femininity through a process of derision and degradation.

Step 1: Humiliation

Figure 50: Feminism as a three-step process

Another ant joins the farm, attempting to compete directly with the ones that mastered it for millennia. 'Women can do anything men can', they claim – but where are the results, the evidence? Only figments of their imagination perhaps, nothing more. This cognitive dissonance in rejecting any degree of inferiority towards the *competing* sex, men, inevitably derails into the slippery-slope of bitterness: if we can't join them, let's at least hate them. Jealousy, potentially the most negative human emotion and rife in the female sex, sets in out of frustration and the procedure to declare *toxic masculinity* as any *excess* of masculinity that males feature in relation to their female counter-parts takes place. A sound strategy to deny all the superior characteristics and traits found in men and claim those as a form of evil. The vilification of male strength is made easier through the true element of toxicity, coming in the form of female aggression. Not through physical strength, because men are superior at that too, but through innuendo, gossip, manipulation, character assassination, bad-mouthing or any other form of poisonous spread of a social miasm that women strove on for thousands of years, seeing it was a means of exercising their power in the tribal environment they seldom left. Women exercise any type of power in a covert manner, destroying their target rather than killing it, as they lack the strength, agility and courage to achieve positive results in direct confrontation. The more radical the feminist, the more bitter, misandrist and toxic they will become – alike insects, the bright hair colors a clear warning sign of the venom to avoid.

Female strength also manifests itself in a widely different manner than that of the male's when concerning positive female traits. For example, women developed an acute sense of self-preservation which was invaluable to ensure the survival of their children. If a woman died it's a lot more likely her children would be butchered too, or simply neglected and prone to failure and misery. When leaving the *female sphere*, that is the realm women inhabited while fulfilling their natural role as care-takers, and entering the *male sphere* in order to compete head-on with men and the role the latter engaged in, women perverted these once positive characteristics into negative ones. Thence, as per **Figure 51**, the feminine characteristic of self-preservation is transformed into cowardice in the realm of masculinity; the maternal care-giving of children mutates into segregation based on tribalistic, superficial traits; the need to control and obsessively protect their young derails into the new phenomenon of *Karenism*; the need to have a man who protects and provides for the woman in the nest quickly converts into the search for a dictatorial nanny-state that satisfies those needs – if they can't marry a man, they will marry the state, one way or the other.

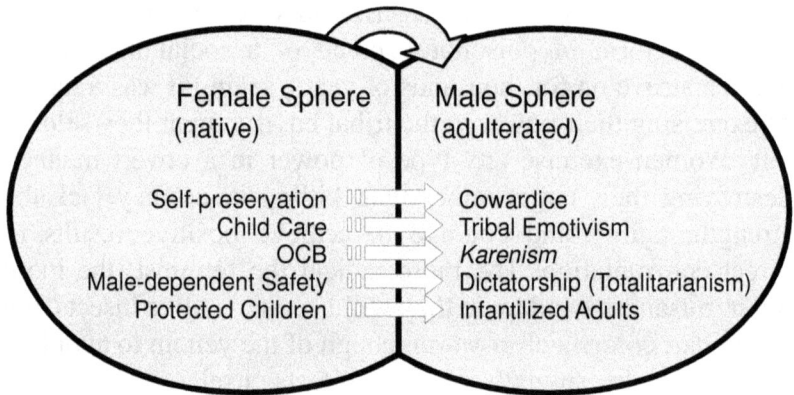

Figure 51: Male and female spheres

METASTASIS

skull and crossbones

Our species, the Homo Sapiens, has been around for 300 thousand years and one of our greatest reasons for success, seen we are the last surviving sub-species of the Homo after all, is the way we harness sexual dimorphism. The fact that we have different morphological characteristics between male and female was a focal point for us in sociological and evolutionary terms. Men used their larger frame, stronger bodies and lack of a womb to center their tasks on resource gathering, fighting and building. This allowed women to remain safe in the tribal environment and devote their attention to birthing, raising and nurturing our young. The latter developed exceptional skills in communication, care-giving, care-taking, decorating (themselves and their surroundings) and multi-tasking due to being inserted in this protected, sheltered setting. It was inefficient to misuse the female's ability to give birth and breastfeed children, as well as any other similar characteristics, since these were acquired as an extension of the female duties.

After many thousands of years, evolution led to the biggest human dichotomy: the female brain in humans is not the same as the male's, therefore women have a different mental framework to men. Women operate under emotional thinking in order to make their decisions. They are hot and cold, accessing all the possible positive and negative emotional impacts, hence becoming extremely indecisive by nature. They matured a type of thinking based on the sheltered and highly social tribal environment, lacking the need to engage in deep rational thinking in order to ensure the survival of the species. Groups that are protected in social environments tend to exhibit underdeveloped characteristics such as lack of risk-taking, conformity, laziness and entitlement – if they are being cared for, why pursue such cumbersome and unwholesome affairs?

Being guided by emotion results in spiritual growth, because the investment made into nurturing and social engagement are indelible to the uniqueness of humanity and our advanced psychology. It's a perilous journey however, and not without an aftermath: the propensity for irrational behavior that results in chaotic decision-making and psychological imbalance. Like with any form of specialization it's not without cost and women are exceedingly poor, if not completely inept, at taking care of themselves without a social infrastructure provided to them by men. There is a reason why every human society and all civilizations have always been patriarchal – as opposed to there being a 'patriarchy', like the tin-foil hat feminists tend to suggest.

One of the clear effects of dwelling so intensely in emotion is also tied to its main source: children. Due to the condition of women bearing and raising their children, an extremely close bond is formed that is referred to as the *motherly instinct* (or *maternal instinct)*. This can be described as the brain-wiring that women naturally have to care, protect and ensure the safety of their offspring. Spirituality is more than emotion, with reason being the proper way to see the Way, the Truth, the Life. With such a heavy investment on the former sensory skill-set, along with power offered to them by weak men, society starts falling victim to what could be described as the *cat-lady syndrome*, where women apply their naturally predominant instinct to nurture fully grown adults under the guise of pity and victimhood.

As seen in **Figure 52**, the instinct that women possess affects their thinking process in an all-encompassing manner, leading women to have an acute sense of control over their children due to these being a cause for constant chaos and disruption – they are humans in development after all. An *obsessive controlling behavior* (OCB) can be observed in women to a much greater degree than in men. Being a *control freak* in the appropriate context, the familial one, is consequently acceptable, but one can instantly foresee the negative impact once transported into positions of power and rule within a society – a foreign context when it comes to the adequateness of such manipulative and dominant tendencies.

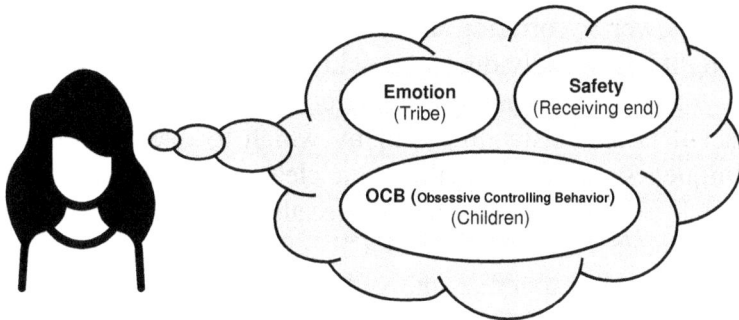

Figure 52: The human female thinking process

Another negative effect is that women will always trade safety over freedom. Due to the complete dependence on men, women never required true freedom, instead relying on men to provide for and protect them. Women had it easy in this regard and as a consequence this removes them from being suitable candidates to choose leaders and make other choices that greatly influence the destiny of a nation – and even civilization at a larger scale. The aforementioned maternal instinct relates to this issue as well, seeing children need safety too. It comes tied to the same need for women to control in a single bundle, as these are the terms of their survival needs.

Upon the shift towards matriarchal societies (**Figure 53**), the female mental framework started redesigning social rules to suit the emotional thinking process, reverting back to an immature, and consequentially primordial, setting. The outcome is a perpetually regressive state taking us back to a very distant past. Social dysgenics, based on the misuse of their motherly instinct, bring about incompetent leaders in both the private and public sector. Freedoms are discarded for the benefit of safety, allowing despot-wannabes to con their way into power by offering all sorts of paradisaical outcomes and delights. The individual is quickly replaced by the herd, with the second appearing to offer safety in sheer numbers, when in fact it is an outstanding tool by which to dissolve the pesky uniqueness of individuality – a clear a prerequisite for true equality. Furthermore, herds are also easier to control and manipulate, revealing the OCB effect in action. All these alterations put together unavoidably result in a chaotic society encrusted with misery, persecution, inequities and also political promiscuity among the ones holding power over the herd.

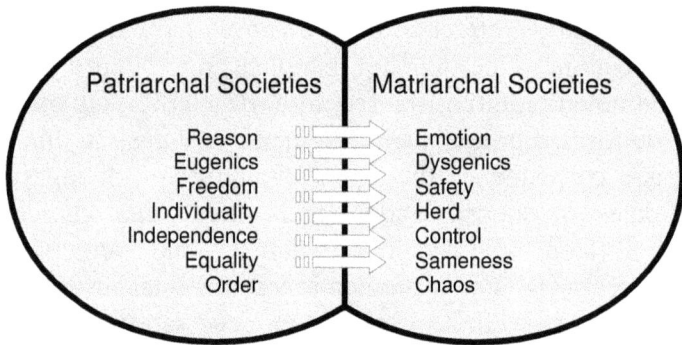

Patriarchal Societies	Matriarchal Societies
Reason	Emotion
Eugenics	Dysgenics
Freedom	Safety
Individuality	Herd
Independence	Control
Equality	Sameness
Order	Chaos

Figure 53: End results of the Matriarchal Shift

The voting process is the primary instrument used to delegate power to those who will ensure their constituents social stability, infrastructures, justice and protection against external threats. Perceived as an essential *right*, it was given to all citizens of nations around the world – certainly all Western nations. Women therefore acquired the power for such choice, putting them in equal footing with men, but without all the struggle, hard-work the latter endured, nor the enterprise they involved themselves in. Through the sameness of Marxism, where any divergent traits of any group, including their failures and successes, are perceived as an act of external disturbance and oppression, feminism vouched to place women in an advantageous position without any of the effort nor the mandatory mental framework. A social miasm ensued, referred to in this book neologistically as the *Matriarchal Shift*, eviscerating the social equilibrium put forth by the Western forefathers, where men ruled through power and authority but also took the brunt of the blame through responsibility and self-sacrifice. If men built, fought, conquered, sailed, scouted, defended, philosophized, debated and innovated, women were the ones on the receiving end of such deluge of gifts and offers – why should both be side-by-side in terms of leadership?

Chivalry in the West was exactly formulated in order to cater for this difference in social status. If women are the weaker sex and depend on men they should submit and serve them, who in turn have the duty to protect and provide for the opposite sex. This was extended into the social norm to treat women in a highly regarded fashion, a manifestation of respect and honor for the female's vulnerability. In the current state of degeneracy, Western countries are now struggling to figure out where and when to use chivalry, a concept that is clearly outdated but seems so natural to us. It's hard to get rid of such habit, but with the present state of affairs it must be done so women can finally be treated as 'equals', even when they are clearly not. Equal rights is the key ingredient of egalitarianism, whereas feminism prefers the *sameness* of Marxism, i.e. the concept of everyone being identical despite gender, race and other personal traits. These are seen as shallow and irrelevant but they are what is presently dictating the current Overton window. If one were to propose offering women perhaps a one-fifth of a men's vote, or removing that ability from the female gender altogether, these would be considered nothing short of heresy, with the evil doer quickly burned at the stake of public opinion. Such suggestion would without doubt spark outrage in any woman's mind, no matter how feminist they consider themselves to be or not. Voting should be perceived under a function of *merit*, not as a legal right as it came to be since the inception of feminism. To women it constitutes *privilege*, because it needs to be *given* to them – gifted and offered by those of the strong sex who fought and died to *earn* it. All in all, only through hard-work voting can be attributed to be a consequence of merit, whereas without it it's nothing more than favor, resulting in an inequal society. If one struggles to agree, due to arrogance or convenience, the solution is simple: have the roles switched by placing women at the elm doing all the hard-work, while men can be the ones inheriting the bonus of being allowed to partake in the societal and civilizational decision-making instead, and no doubt will be left standing.

THE MODERN WOMAN

from beauty to ugliness

Traditionally women had a submissive role towards men, exposing them to a potential bad husband, and any consequences that could come from a bad marriage. For this reason they had to take into consideration whether they trusted this person and if their love for the candidate, with whom they'd form a future partnership, was deep enough. However this metric has been lost with the empowerment of women, especially from a financial perspective. More often than not, modern women will make disastrous choices in the firm belief they have plenty of other options in case the relationship they got themselves into doesn't work out. As a last resort they can always marry the state by latching onto a very generous system of welfare if the divorce settlement isn't enough. These are in themselves extremely prejudicial against men, including the ascription of child custody that falls the majority of time to the mother.

But even if we are to exclude marriage and children, modern women still have a false sense of security and independence that invariably leads to poor partner choices. The loss of *submission* as a gauge to measure if a woman really likes a man is nothing but another harmful outcome of feminism. A woman could otherwise carefully evaluate whether the man in question would be worthy of pursuit for a more serious affair and the risk of pregnancy. The loss of such a powerful defense mechanism should have led to skepticism towards the ideology in question but instead it was ignored. *Monkey-branching*, i.e. the act of switching partners with high frequency, has been praised as *slut culture*. In the event the subsequent carelessness leads to this type of *slutty* woman finding herself pregnant, there is always the *pro-choice* movement, providing the ability to 'erase' the mistake through abortion – nothing short of murder, even though they deny it. The other alternative is single motherhood, but both are praised as affirming the empowerment of women, their immense success inescapably resulting in dying alone, bitter and miserable – fully guaranteed.

Starting with the latter, single parenting is always a bad idea as an option and should only be considered as a last resort when the relationship fractured – after all the steps to make it succeed were taken. When using traditional methods of match-making there is always a chance that the progenitors move apart from each other after several years, but praise for single motherhood only results in displicence and the massive increase in couples separating through divorce. The option of choosing to keep the child, or children, will inevitably lead to the need for a search of a partner that provides resources, safety and companionship as opposed to a true love bond, with extremely high odds of that choice being very poor and more based on haste and conformity rather than happiness. Consideration must also be taken into the possibility of an unpaired woman failing to find a partner that is fine with a 'ready-made family'.

The other alternative is that of aborting the child and resetting the woman's life choices, as if that were possible. To begin with women are exceedingly emotional beings and the idea that any woman could destroy the life they are carrying inside them, no matter what stage of gestation, without severe psychological and emotional damage is laughable at best. In fact, *pro-choice* is nothing more than pro-murder, and deep inside her female psyche the woman that destroys the possibility of having that child will always carry this within her. Like Christopher Hitchens (1949 – 2011) said, "If life doesn't start at conception, then when *does* it start"? Feminists will attempt to attribute value to life in the womb *only* if there is a heartbeat, or maybe if a brain is visible in the scan – or at the very least it should be required the shape of a human at its earliest embryonic stage. All these arguments are nothing more than excuses to legitimize murder.

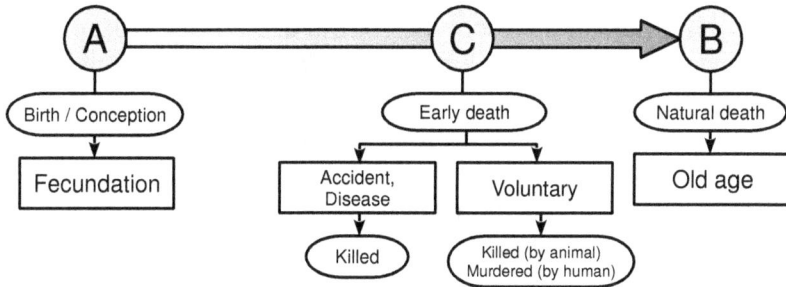

Figure 54: The true (and only) definition of life, through representation of the life-cycle

Life has to be perceived as a cycle, whether it's mammal or any other type: animal or vegetable. In the case of animal life, the cycle starts at fecundation when the male, who contributes to the procedure with a *gamete* (a reproductive single-cell organism) called the *spermatozoon*, mates with a fertile female, who in turn contributes with a single-cell organism called the *ovum*. A *zygote* is produced as the end result of both cells fusing together through fertilization. The latter will then subdivide repeatedly into a cell mass that will grow to become an embryo inside the uterus. Therefore life starts at fecundation, that is when the *zygote* is created, since there is no other stage that we can assign a beginning point to. Looking at **Figure 54** we can see in abstract form life as a cycle – a process of self-growth, aging and death. The endpoint *B*, natural death, will be met if there is no interference during the journey, otherwise endpoint *C* represents a precocious death.

This could be caused by either accident, disease or an external agent (another living organism), with the last falling into the classification of *being killed*.

If a human therefore dies of old age no-one will refer to that event in a form of attributing blame to any of the said factors. But if a third-party interferes, let's say a lion mauls a person to death, then we attribute blame to the causal agent. If the agent is a human being whom, out of his own volition, stopped the life-cycle purposely, then we refer to that act as *murder*. It bears no significance *when* the voluntary act occurs during the cycle, as long as it is perpetrated by a human-being capable of rational thought and objective decision making.

If a plant is pulled out of its roots and left to die, we consider the agent that pulled it to have killed the plant, even though the vegetable life-form will never have a heart or a brain at any stage of its development. The simple fact is that once the life-cycle has started the only way to end it is to halt the process by killing it, or alternatively letting it age and reach the end of its natural cycle. In any other scenario there must be a factor that led to an early death and, in case the factor involves a being in possession of reason, because we can't place blame on a wolf, an earthquake or a disease at the same level, responsibility must be assigned.

Even with the lack of pregnancy, female empowerment directs women towards a life of promiscuity, which is seen as emancipation for females that have been bound to tradition and social norms since the dawn of mankind. Once more a trap is set to offer women a harmful solution that leads to emotional scarring. Humans are biological creatures and as such are shaped by nature based on their evolutionary roles. Women, as the ones in ownership of a womb, carried the obligation to ensure the survival of the species through self-preservation and raising their brethren, always under the protection of men, who in turn exposed themselves to acquire resources and build shelter. This agreement is in fact the most used among mammals and results in males being the *predators* in the dating game, whereas females are the *prey*. Men's aggression is imperative in the pursuit for the qualifying woman, or women, whom in turn will analyze the man's strength, characterized by height, muscular mass, age, skill and intellect. Women have a lot to lose by mating with a weak man that displays lack of facial symmetry, intelligence, social status or lack of resources, as being impregnated by such male would incur a high risk of failure due to bad genes, starvation, precarious shelter and lack of safety. Such woman would have to not only take care of herself, but also be in charge of taking care of her children without anyone else involved.

The value of women therefore lies in giving themselves to a single, high quality specimen who will in turn reward her with a good, stable life. With female empowerment, this factor seems to have evaporated – but is there more to it then meets the eye? A man is considered a *stud* if he is desirable and is able to mate with a lot of women because of the principle that women are defensive and have a lot to lose, as explained above. In *slut culture* this factor doesn't change much, because women will still flock to give themselves away to the most attractive, healthy, wealthy men within reach. This culture of hypergamy only make women more accessible to these men and prevents the less desirable males from getting a female partner. It also turns women into *sluts*, not studs, because once women, being the *prey*, are easy to get, they lose the value in the dating game (**Figure 55**). They never *had* to chase after men, which means they will lose value by offering themselves easily, whereas the *studs* that carousel through them happily acquire what the other males cannot. One could say that women still maintain that power over the weak, less attractive males but they will lose that leverage with the studs they *could* have partnered with in first place.

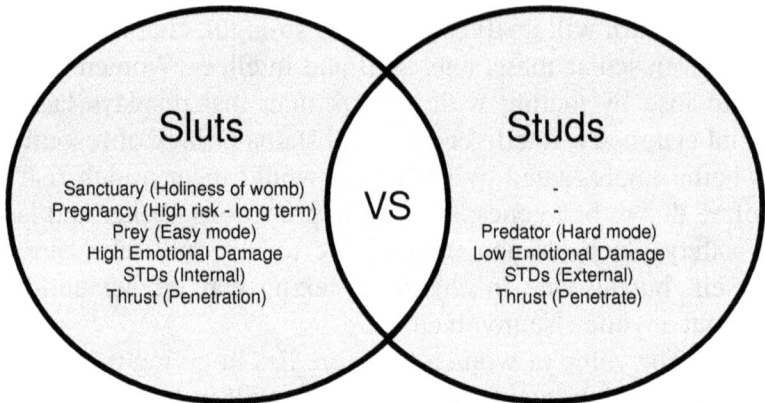

Figure 55: The outcomes from male and female promiscuity

However there are further problems beyond acquiring a man for resources and safety. Women that have a high 'body-count' lose their respectability tied to the sanctity of the womb. Anyone would reckon if they were to find out one of their progenitors had been a porn star and had engaged in sexual relations with hundreds of members of the opposite sex, the choice would always fall onto the father. It's not that most people would be fine with knowing there is pornographic material out there with their father on it, but rather that had the mother been the one, a greater deal of shame would ensue. We still came from our mother's womb after all, not our father's and the prospect of knowing that path had been traversed by hundreds of men is a lot less endearing than whatever our father's misgivings may have been.

A woman that has multiple partners will also suffer vaginal wall stretching which, although controversial especially during the current Overton window where the shadow of feminism looms over everything, after many sexual encounters with different men there is the propensity for the female eventually preferring a partner that is well-sized sexually, leading to the possibility of having difficulty in enjoying sexual pleasure with a male of a smaller size – aspect that she could disregard later in life, but why should she? In effect a large amount of partners will result in a much greater possibility of sexually transmitted infections that are a lot more troublesome in women than in men due to their internal nature.

Last but not least, women are much more prone to suffer from severe emotional scarring than men, which in the long run, after many failed relationships and rejections, leads to neurosis, bitterness and paranoia. A woman that waded through many sexual partners will have great difficulty in finding peace and resolution in settling down with someone after so many experiences. Looking into her past, there was always a better jaw, a better six-pack, a more pleasurable love-muscle, a more intelligent, wealthier or polite man. Adding to this the doubt whether will he cheat, will he lie, will he harm her also accrues out of having gone previously through bad experiences. All these and more thoughts will roam forever inside the victim of slut behavior. Though not immune, men have a good deal better time discarding these scars, but not in such severeness.

In the end of the day men need to chase, so it's *difficult* to get women, thus their value is in *conquest*. Women just accept which men to be with, so it's *easy* to get them, hence their value being in *resistivity*. Men prefer quantity, women prefer quality – until feminism broke this logic, that is.

THE MODERN MAN

from strength to weakness

The concept of *Blue Pill* comes from the movie The Matrix (1999), where the protagonist, Neo, is offered the choice to embrace the reality just revealed to him, with such pill resulting in him forgetting everything he learned and going back into the slumbering sleep of quotidian life. The *Red Pill* offered the opposite result: Neo would become fully aware of the fact that the whole world as he perceived it was in fact a simulation. Logically, these two terms were brought over into our modern social lexicon to reflect the idea that men either accept or deny the obvious facts about our society in respect to sex. If a man is indeed aware of the fact that he is at severe disadvantage as an individual, solely out of being born male, due to the increase of gynocentrism and hypergamy in the social environment, he is considered *Red Pilled*. If unaware, or just in plain denial, of all the contemporary benefits the opposite sex enjoys, he will be referred to as *Blue Pilled*. A third term was brought over in addition to the former two called *Black Pilled*, which refers to *Red Pilled* men that go into the downward spiral of depression, dejection and disbelief – these are the ones that go a step further and have the greatest propensity to be misogynistic.

The three pills (**Figure 56**) can therefore be associated with the state of mental awareness of men in relation to how uneven social norms and rules have become since the inception of feminism. Men are in fact negotiating a mine-field, where at any given moment they could end up dismembered or even destroyed at whim of a member of the opposite sex. Whether the man in question is an Alpha (leader), a PUA (pick-up-artist) or an Incel (involuntary celibate), he will have to fit himself into this societal schism by choosing which one pill to take.

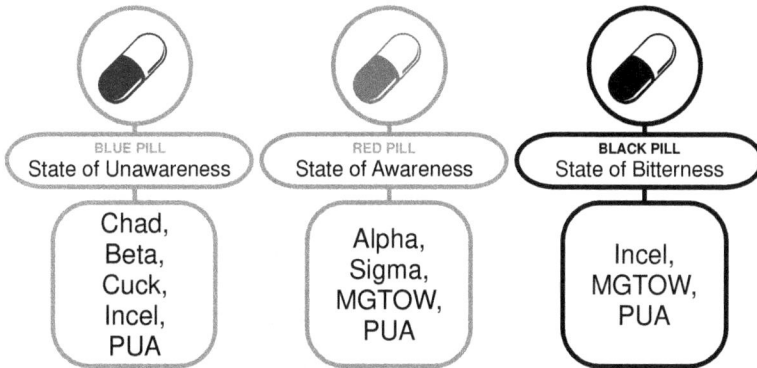

BLUE PILL State of Unawareness	RED PILL State of Awareness	BLACK PILL State of Bitterness
Chad, Beta, Cuck, Incel, PUA	Alpha, Sigma, MGTOW, PUA	Incel, MGTOW, PUA

Figure 56: The three pills feminism served men

The old adage *nice guys finish last* could not be more self-unaware. With the advent of the shift of modern Western societies into an artificial matriarchal design, we can clearly take notice of how women truly see *nice* men. Women always had a submissive role that privileged them with protection, safety and resources, thence being devoted to finding the strongest male that could provide for them. If women are programmed to find a partner with those characteristics, then an unsuitable partner will be perceived as *weak,* not *nice.* A strong man is a woman's *king,* a leader that deserves her subservience and devotion, unlike a weak man who she will perceive as a *servant,* while seeing herself as the queen. A man that presents himself as *nice* is actually bowing to the woman, relinquishing any authority or leadership over to her. Any queen needs a her own king, not a lowly subordinate.

It has to be pointed out that strength in a man does not equate physical prowess necessarily. As a matter of fact male strength is a closer synonym to confidence, intelligence, integrity, hard work, diligence and leadership. Feminists will use the straw man argument that there is no need for oafish, thuggish, macho type of men and that society has evolved beyond the need for them, but this is widely misleading since not only these men are indeed still absolutely substantive to the functioning and improvement of social infrastructure and the gathering of resources, but also the fact that men were always both the *brawn* and also the *brain.*

The mass presence of weak, beta males is an artifact of modern gynocentric societies, comprising of another two types of males in addition to this one: the rebellious MGTOW (Men Going Their Own Way) loner and the rise of the high-testosterone, patriarchal migrant male. A matriarchal society designed by feminism produces these three kinds of men (see **Figure 57**), which in turn results in a fractured, weak and divided society. Single motherhood is a major factor in the production of beta males, who grow up without strong father figures and more often than not engage in the practice of simping. These tend to be overly nice and soft towards women in an attempt to establish a relationship with them, while embracing any feminist views that are harmful to themselves and instead beneficial to the women they court, such as *fat acceptance, believe all women* and similar. The practice of *white knighting* is also distinctive of these weak men, because they were groomed, sometimes smothered, by their mothers, with these beta males instinctively attempting to protect women under any circumstances, even when females are in the wrong. They often offer an abundance of their own resources, usually in the form of monetary value, to women that supply them with any sort of frivolities, including online messaging or 'private' nude photos.

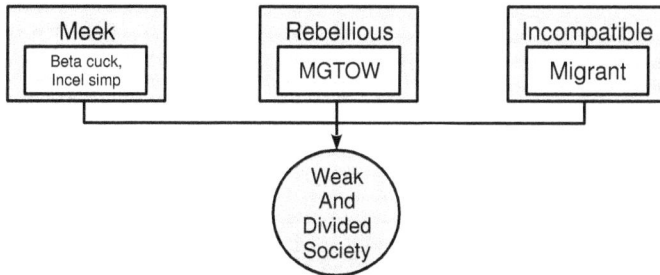

Figure 57: Feminism creates to three types of men

The MGTOW men are the rebels that, being self-assertive, prefer to redirect their potential in acquiring resources to their own benefit, investing in their presentation, fitness, personal grooming and property. Disappointed with the present societal model, they defer all personal attention and energy that could have been possibly directed to a female partner, onto their own happiness and success. This often also implies a greater degree of isolation, with a 'better safe then sorry' approach. This is justified due to a lot of men that embrace the traditional stereotype of 'married with children' under a post-modernistic society, also frequently ending up isolated after divorce – but with their resources depleted in favor of the ex-wife (or ex-partner) and a lot of child support, perhaps even alimony, in their expense list.

The third and last type of men feminism produces is derived from the paradoxical mass-importation of patriarchal males from third-world countries, which feminists pursue in a typically female dysfunctional manner: due to a sense of pity towards individuals that suffer the results of their own civilizational incompetence and corresponding demise, under the *maternal instinct* women endeavor to rescue and babysit these third-worlders. Modern women can treat these men as if dealing with children all they want, but when they reach numbers large enough, they will inevitably become those very feminist's greatest foe, owing to these men's utmost incompatibility with matriarchal concepts and values.

Further, subject to the natural order of human biology, women mature earlier than men. However because the peak of their fertility, beauty, sexuality and vitality comes at an younger age, they end up misusing it the vast majority of times. The odd exception is to remain traditional and devote herself to a man of high quality. Men on the other hand, mature later so they can afford to be obtuse and empty-headed when young, as they have more time to reach the peak of their maturity. There is a lot of experience that comes with the latter so there is a lot more value there, hence the preference of women to having an older partner that is established, mature and displays a higher level of intelligence – before Feminism butchered the whole concept that is, and sold to women the idea of offering themselves away to useless younger men in a party culture. Adding insult to injury, by telling them to focus on careers instead of starting a family – family which they will unavoidably attempt to pursue in a rush by the time their ovum start drying up – feminism sure got the noose around the modern woman's neck.

Emotional damage in dating is worse for women who are left with more scars, but conversely men suffer from the lack of ability to pair with young women at the peak of their appeal. The ones that subsist in the search of a relationship turn out partnering with older, less desirable women, whom will have in their memories the experiences of good times and happiness with the younger men they chased superficial relationships with. Were women to choose the traditional path, and had they favored family over career and partying, those memories would be made with the man they tied themselves to – plus the couple's emotional bond, and the one with their children, would gain from it. Instead due to such social experiments that deform the natural order of things, overall the modern man has to content himself with leftover-women, often single mothers or aged women filled with neurosis and emotional damage – or no women at all.

THE GYNOCENTRIC COLLAPSE

men die, women cry

Through the process of selective filtering, women undermine male achievements by placing focus on the negative aspects and discarding the positive ones. This becomes much more evident when women use this process to judge, and condemn, successful patriarchal designs, with the more obvious instance being the Christian West. Every step in the evolution ladder is scrutinized under the highly reductive lens of *good* and *evil*. Even necessary *evil* actions, like the ones that can be perceived as indispensable steps in civilizational development and growth, are used to attack the 'patriarchy' as the root of societal impairment. Let's take the example of slavery, which was ever-present throughout human history in all societies and cultures in some way or another: Christians are chastised for engaging in such practices but never praised for actually having abolished, and then exported and enforced this new ruling world-wide. In fact without such measures the very women berating Western Christian males would not have such standards by which to judge them with. In reality it's absolutely obligatory to engage in the said *evil* before recognizing and bringing it into the global ethos, and subsequently program it into the collective subconscious. No other culture or civilization had done so before, so what credibility can be given to women for such poor judgment skills?

Women underpin their effort at refactoring the naturally built patriarchal human societies into artificial matriarchies through arrogance – they perceive themselves as competent and capable without any expertise, knowledge or evidence. Men can look back and see all that they built, innovated, discovered and fought for. Men are meritful, women privileged. The latter thus undervalue men's achievements through an emotion that is exceedingly dominant in them and has been brought up before here – jealousy. They ravel on criticisms and judgmental views to make up for all they lack in terms of worth and value. It's an unequivocal fact that female Homo-sapiens have been around for as long as their male counter-parts, defeating any feminist arguments to excuse failure or underachievement. Women's role in the human evolutionary process has been very distinctly entrenched and defined as the dwellers of the nest, resulting in a dependence on men, who would gather resources and provide them with shelter. To assume with great hubris that they could simply flick a switch and compete head-on in the execution of masculine affairs is beyond cognitive dissonance – it's sheer arrogance and stupidity.

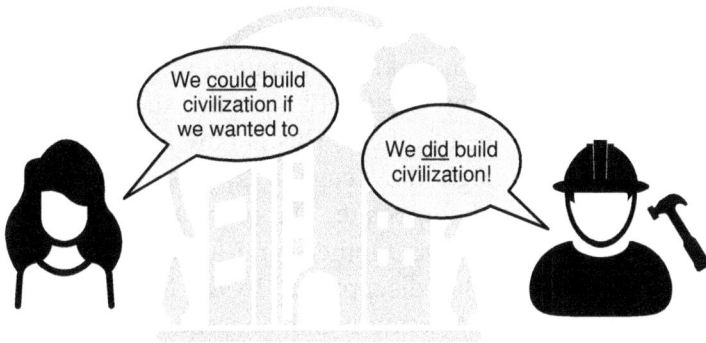

Figure 58: Arrogance vs confidence

Men built the Ethos through prostrating themselves before a higher authority that offered the same level of love, compassion and protection for them as the one they offered to women. Under the doctrine of self-sacrifice, which led to the genesis of the hero archetype, men always surrendered their value in the name of principals, achievement, and of course the survival of their partners and offspring. This behavior organically committed men to positions of power to establish social cohesion and regulate its design – all part of the natural order of things. Men are therefore fit to occupy roles of power, authority and responsibility.

Under the Matriarchal Shift, society traversed a balanced formula onto a gynocentric one, emphasizing female interests over mutual interests. Allied with the Marxist formula of oppression under feminism, women constituted themselves as the victims and the female pathos started taking over the original male ethos. A deep immersion into self-pity and a quest for victimhood ensued and is still undergoing, until this sea of piranhas leaves nothing left. Since women are used to being provided with shelter and resources, and therefore are the primary beneficiaries of the male sacrifice, they developed pathological narcissism, making them unfit to rule society. The reality is they will always selfishly prioritize themselves while expecting the sacrifice of others. This is how feminism leads to inequality, even though they engage in false advertising by claiming it procures the opposite. The original role that women had through femininity, as mothers and lovers, as care-givers and care-takers, is highly disapproved by the feminist ideology, resulting in women neglecting it and, consequently, the *modern woman* has become little more then a social parasite.

There are plenty of examples throughout history where, mostly due to war, societies shifted towards gynocentrism, such as Sparta and the Vikings, which quickly led to their collapse. Men, through the hero archetype, are masochistic and engage in self-sacrifice, whereas women, due to the need for self-preservation, employ self-commiseration. The former engaged in a strategy that has an abundance of evidence to support its success, unlike with the latter who have nothing besides claims and a delusional sense of confidence.

CHAPTER 10

Back to the Cave

FIRST STEPS TOWARDS REGRESSION

 # not all

Women defend groups based on their motherly instinct. Instead of pitying the wounded duckling or the puppy missing a leg, now that they have power in Western societies, they focus their pity onto social groups based on basic tribalistic, low-IQ differentials – such as race, ethnicity, gender, sexual orientation, religion, etc. But the truth is these groups are pitied out of inferiority. At subconscious level, feminists and Woke activists that advocate for such ideas with foolish, if not downright imbecilic slogans know this.

If one were to single out a group and remove it from the human historical context, that is, if we were to imagine a racial or ethnic group never existed, how would that affect the course of human history? Imagine the Black African went extinct twenty thousand years ago – how would that have affected our history? The obvious negative effects are those that involve sports and music. There wouldn't be such varied types of beat-based music such as rap or hip-hop. Plus the world record for the one-hundred meters sprint or the marathon would be not as good, and certainly sports in general would not have as good quality. But aside from this, what influence would there be? What would we lose? Can one figure out any other clear benefits such group of peoples provided us with?

Conversely, there would be great advantages if such were to happen. Wherever large contingents of the Black African can be found in the world, there tend to be serious problems with crime, savagery, brutality, incivility. Take Brazil, USA, Caribbean islands and, obviously, Sub-Saharan Africa – wouldn't these places instantly benefit from the lack of such problems? Not to mention the fact that this land could then be utilized by civilized groups that would add much to human civilization, which is exactly what happened in territories with a low degree of native population, such as North America and Australasia.

East-Asian cultures seem to be quite frontal about this facts and tend not engage in the pathetic *politically correct* behavior that Westerners have embraced, all due to the Matriarchal Shift. Extending the example to Islam and terrorism, certainly not all Muslims are terrorists, neither do all Islamic countries have the death penalty for such trivial affairs as homosexuality. But again if one were to try to engage in a similar exercise and imagine that instantly, without any action related to violence or suppression, all Muslims in the world adopted any other religion – it could be Christianity, Hinduism, Buddhism, or any other – wouldn't the world see itself rid of so many problems to do with intolerance, bigotry and, most of all, the violence of terrorism?

Plus, what disadvantages would there be from losing Islam? What has this specific religion contributed to the world? Aside from the absurdity of the tall-tale of the supposed

Islamic Golden Age and the 1001 Islamic Inventions (which are inventions in the true sense as they are nothing more than complete fabrications and distortions of historical facts), what would have humanity lost? A Muslim Algerian historian in the seventeenth century recorded the first successful attempt of flying in human history by Abbas Ibn Firnas (810 – 887 A.D.), a Mulsim inventor that lived in the then colonized by Islam Iberian Peninsula. However, Leonardo Da Vinci (1452 – 1519 A.D.) who lived a full century before the Muslim historian had come up with the design for a glider, making it possible, if not entirely reasonable, that the idea would have been somewhat plagiarized once he became acquainted with it. Moreover, there are actual records of Da Vinci's design (**Figure 59**), whereas nothing aside from the claim of the Muslim Algerian historian was presented – one would have to take his account purely at face value, which is a terrible way of accounting for historical and scientific facts.

Similar problems can be found with claims regarding the Persian scholar and mathematician Ibn Musa al-Khwarizmi (780 – 850 A.D.), revered by Muslims as the father of algebra. He certainly wrote the compendium of Algebra that was later adopted by Europeans who in turn achieved great progress in the same field. But the obvious question arises: if there were five-hundred years of this Islamic Golden Age (during which al-Kwarizmi lived), then why no else in this outstanding era gave continuity to his work? Five centuries is plenty of time for many other brilliant minds to manifest themselves – where was the 'Islamic Age of Enlightenment'? Hundreds, if not thousands, of such individuals can be quoted during the corresponding era in Europe. To further the problem, the Ancient Greek philosopher Pythagoras of Samos (570 – 495 B.C.), along with others of that time period, had already engaged in algebraic work. In fact, the first evidence of algebra can be traced back to the Babylonians almost two thousands years before Christ.

Leonardo da Vinci's glider sketch circa 1510 A.D.

Al-Khwārizmī's compendium of Algebra circa 820 A.D.

Babylonian tablet listing two Pythagorean triples circa 1800 B.C.

Pythagoras of Samos
Ancient Greek philosopher and mathematician circa 570 – 495 B.C.

Figure 59: Claims for Islamic Inventions

Still, Muslims perpetuate the claim and pretend the merit relates to them. An identical situation is being lived today with the use of Afrocentrism to hijack other peoples history and present it as Black African achievements. No merit should be taken away from anyone, including the Persian mathematician who humbly gave credit to the Hindu monks in India he took a lot of knowledge from to form his compendium. Indeed he appropriately, and originally, named what we call today Arabic numerals (as European were honest and named them after the people they learned them from) as simply Hindu numerals. But the real question that needs to be asked is, would he have not achieved this outside Islam? In simpler words, was Islam itself conducive to such an astounding level of human achievement or the exact opposite, resistant?

The point being made is that history speaks for itself and the achievements, or lack thereof, of cultures, ethnic groups, religions, empires is what should lead to the conclusion of how salutary or valuable they were to human civilizational growth. If Islam had invented the airplane – which even Da Vinci isn't claimed to have done, since at best it would have been a glider, which is altogether different from an airplane and is exactly what Ibn Firnas would have invented but didn't – wouldn't the Islamic world have made use of this outstanding achievement and apply it to warfare, commerce, etc? If Nubian Africans were so successful as to build the Egyptian pyramids, instead of the Coptic Egyptians as history accurately reports, wouldn't these level of entrepreneurial spirit and advanced mindset reflect on other accomplishments to this very day?

At the end of the day, without the two most successful religions in the World's history, Christianity and Buddhism, where would our species be at? If we are to remove Christianity from history, the modern world would be straight out of the window. It's where everything *modern* started once Christian Europeans released themselves of the Islamic choke-hold and connected to Asia, like two wires sparking an ignition for the current era. Most societies would be prehistoric stone-age cultures and the remaining would be living in a medieval setting at best. No cars or airplancs, printcd books and magazines, human rights and animals rights, the rule of law, the sovereignty of the state and the individual. In reality there is so much to reference it would take a whole book to describe all the advances and innovations made by Christian imperialism and colonialism that the entire planet directly benefits from.

CULTURAL DEPRAVITY

the shallow drown in deep waters

Another phenomenon that arose from the Matriarchal Shift is the predominance of the use of emotion instead of reason to engage in social design. Naturally, women will always refer to the traits that they are more comfortable with and have an expertise on, therefore replacing logic and rational thought, that is dominant in men, with feelings and emotions. Unlike men, women guide themselves using their motherly instinct, which albeit indelible to the evolution of the species, is completely inappropriate and adulterant when applied outside it's original context: the familial environment where there is an emotional bond and intimacy between the parties involved.

Factoring in women's dominance in modern Western societies, we end up with copious levels of a *spoiled brat syndrome*, i.e. a societal disorder where children are overly protected and sheltered, leading them to become infantilized adults, or fully grown individuals that behave like spoiled brats, constantly throwing fits, tantrums and screaming their hearts out in order to get things done their way. This is a clear side-effect of the *poisoned apple of Marxism*, also known as feminism. Human females, who spent 300 thousand years in the nest under the protection of the men who built civilization for them, suddenly find themselves a platform they transform

into their test-bed for how society should function. By applying
the only formula they are familiar with, that of care giving,
they reduce society at large to a cradle. Allied to this the fact
that feminism stems from a socialist ideology, it's easy to
identify how the idealistic view of the world where everyone is
happy (except for the slaves who have to work the fields doing
all the hard work) results in cultural depravity. Societies that
suffer from this problem are riddled with the abundance of
overgrown babies and stupidity and become places where
parasitism and ignorance strive.

The lack of exposure to hardship and difficulties leads
to even the minor upset being labeled a *micro-aggression* by
the younger, so called snowflake, generations. To make things
worse, the large-scale dysfunctional behavior exhibited by
them weaken society substantively, eventually downgrading
them to third-world nations. These Woke cultists privilege
opinion and preference over reality, a clear legacy of post-
modernists, post-structuralists and existentialists such as Sartre,
Foucault and Derrida. Filled with sheer hubris, these
generations revolt into civilizational collapse, under the burden
of redesigning and restructuring social norms and conventions,
after rejecting and destroying anything their forefathers built.

The procurement of divinity is no more and objectivity
is replaced with subjectivity, reality with opinion, logic with
preference. The quest for a better World is too much for such
small minds deprived of knowledge, having little ability to
reason and extreme difficulty in employing critical thought.
Degeneracy ensues followed by bratty, or even primate-like
behavior where animality abounds. There is no down-and-dirty
solution for these current trend of snow-flakiness, but the
enforcement of military conscription for a year, or maybe
having the members of such failed generations working in a

farm under supervision – perhaps even sending them on a humanitarian mission to a third-world country to help starving children, build schools or infra-structure for the same amount of time? Certainly it wouldn't fix everything, but it would greatly solidify these coming-of-age individuals character and humbleness before awarding them the power to vote, exercise a position in public office or function, and even enter university. It could be that these degenerate spoiled losers would just become more self-aware and realize how good they have it before taking everything for granted, roaming the streets in the name of a better world when they already live in it.

When a society is dominated by cultural depravity and emotional retardation, extremist views tend to be predominant because they are a product of such backward irrational antics. Views that provide solace to simple minds constitute comforting lies, diametrically opposing the search for answers within the respect and honor their ancestors deserve, even if causing inconvenient truths to be unveiled. Under the duress of the matriarchal shift and its overbearing rules and rulers, several forms of emotional extremism started taking over. *Wokeness* is nothing more than feminism on steroids, appealing mostly to opportunists – before being hunters humans started as scavengers after all, and the more primitive of our kind will be unable to avoid the solace of mediocrity and dependence.

In the 1970s terms such *transvestite, transsexual, cross-dresser, queer* and *lady-boy* started becoming popular as the aftermath of societal changes taking place and, whether we agree with their end purpose or not, these expressions tended to reflect the true meaning behind them. But under the present conditions of emotional extremism, redefining these words became priority, extending some of them into the realm of subjectivity. So any of the terms above are now compacted into *gender identity* and most fall into the *transgender* category as can be seen in **Figure 60**. By transferring such meanings from something that is tangible within the social environment – and the corresponding physical interactions within it – into the mind, the preference, the opinion, they can emote themselves into existence. Furthermore, the spoiled brats that impose and enforce these neologisms onto the social fabric through means of coercion, name-calling and throwing the typical childish tantrums, acquire a great deal of power, which is always a predilection of people that exhibit such radical conduct. The Woke mythology in this cult of dejects is intertwined with victim status as a means to climb up the ladder of significance and relevance.

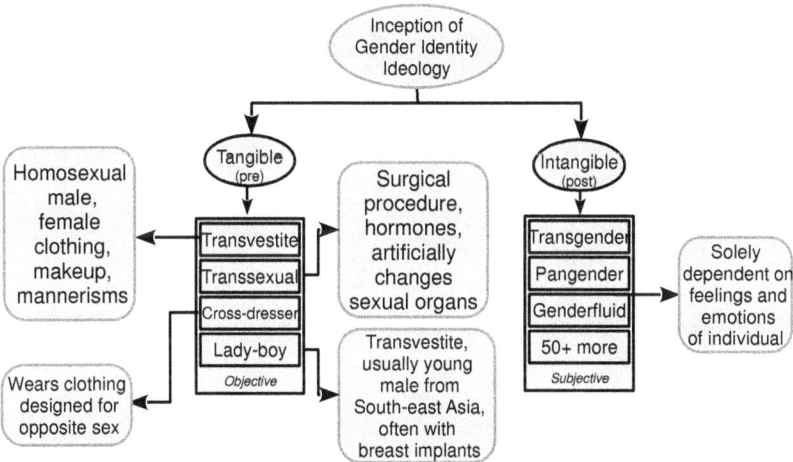

Figure 60: Gender Identitarianism

The formula of *gender identity* cannot be described even by its most fervorous followers of the Woke cult, as doing so would invariably lead to the erasure of whatever whimsical new identity a single individual might cosplay themselves as, since it's a mere product of one's imagination and it relates in no way to anything biological or objective – not even the reproductive system as erroneously assumed by most. In truth, if one can use such words among these incoherent concepts, an individual can identify as a bird, a cake, a furry (person that wears a costume called a *fursuit* that conveys their identity) or even a demon. One can even identify as transracial as the options are limitless.

One can deny these emotion extremists referring to them as they demand, but not without being harassed by the loud noise, *doxing* and the persecution that will follow, something that is hardly typical of open-minded, tolerant types. But what about the oppression factor? What about the suffering of the individual not being treated as he should? Is the lack of usage of appropriate pronouns not a cause to claim derision, bad faith, ill intent? Even lack of manners could be brought into the argument.

To solve the conundrum, we must first bring up the notion of *common-sense*, which can be defined as the general acceptance of certain social norms that any individual can comprehend and accept through basic social interactions. If one is to deviate from these, a justification needs to be added. Referring to **Figure 61**, a logical connection can be established between the threshold of civic behavior, i.e. what is to be expected from a fully functioning member of society by default, and what can be considered privilege, or a special way of treating someone under specific circumstances. As an example, one may be inclined to treat a judge by "your honor" when in a court of law, but that procedure disappears once interacting with the same individual in the middle of the street.

The same would apply to a students treatment of a professor inside an education establishment and the outside it; a police officer while on duty and off-duty, and so on and so forth.

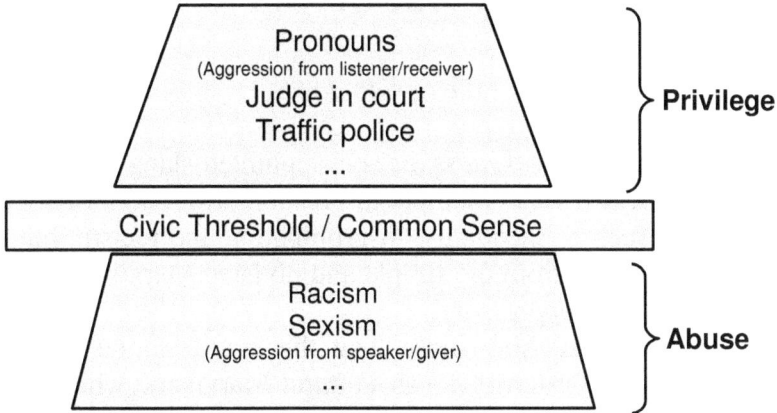

Figure 61: The domain of common-sense

If such social and communal conditions don't arise then the standard diagnostic is that these made-up, imposed pronouns are nothing more than privilege, because they lie beyond normal social convention and therefore common sense. Such enforcement is not warranted and will constitute a violation of civil rights of the individual being coerced into using such pronouns against their will. This can be seen as a clear breach of one's personal freedom of speech, which is to say the express route towards a fascistic society. Commanding others to do as we tell them in the name of freedom is equivalent of murdering in the name of life. Gender identity is nothing more than a children's playground, impregnating society with much greater racial awareness in society, social media, movies, advertising campaigns, etc.

WOKE LADDER OF OPPRESSION

the upside-down

The definition of *wokeness*, as self-appointed slang originating from Black America, attempts to presume awareness of social problems such as inequality, discrimination and racism, but in reality it derives from the simple and divisive Marxist equation of *oppressed vs oppressors*.

This is nothing more than the manifestation of neo-Marxism (also referred to as cultural-Marxism), which is a form of socialism that, as per extension of classical-Marxism blended with feminism, attempts to wrap all evils of society in the typical over-simplistic emotional understanding that females possess on such affairs. This *feel-goodism*, meaning simple solutions for complex problems, ends in the prevalence of emotions over reason, feelings over facts.

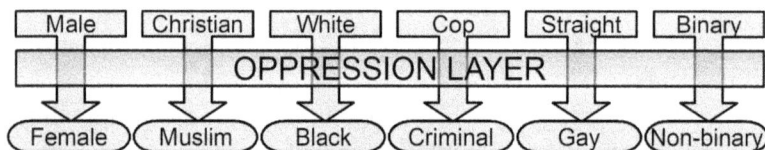

Male	Christian	White	Cop	Straight	Binary

OPPRESSION LAYER

Female	Muslim	Black	Criminal	Gay	Non-binary

Figure 62: Oppression ladder of neo-Marxism

As can be seen in **Figure 62**, race, gender, sexual orientation, gender identity, religion, disability, etc. become the end-point to identify the groups of people, only to then order and neatly pack them in a chain of *oppression* – or to put it simply, victimhood. This exercise in condescending bigotry pities the groups that fail the most, attempting to elevate them to a higher condition through privilege because they lack the merit to do so on their own.

The misconception that Christianity is weak grew alongside the rise of atheism. Adolf Hitler himself showed profound disdain for this religion because he saw advantage in the much greater display of strength from the likes of Islam. However history shows us quite the opposite: Christianity built the modern world and is at the forefront of medical, scientific, technological and social advancement. The reason for this is it provides humans with the ethos to strive, to achieve sophistication and success due to orienting and moving us towards divinity, and thereby away from reducing us to just primates. Islam on the other hand relies on animal strength of brutality by way of conquest and authoritative proclamations and edicts and little else, hence its lack of civilizational success. Atheism relies on the dehumanization of people, transforming societies into machines with humans as mere cogs serving its operation. In fact Christianity is strong, not weak and any misgivings regarding any acts of slaughter, conquest or violence within this faith can be clearly perceived as necessary evils that sophisticated humans must go through to reject evil – certainly after being saturated by its consequences.

The Bible teaches to judge people based on their behavior instead, not superficial traits. This is the exact opposite of the currently ethical remodeling that is occurring in the Western World, with tribalistic, divisive logic categorizing people based on what 'bucket' (or tribe) they fall on. It's however advantageous to judge people based on their actions, ideas, behavior and not what they look like or what they claim to be because the former are the cause of critical consequences to society, whether may they be positive or negative, whether they bring good or harm.

Unlike with the Moderates (Liberals, Conservatives, Centrists), the neo-Marxists opt to label people with tags and use that as a starting point to access their merits, virtues or victimhood. Black Africans, for example, are the most highly ethnocentric race due to lack of ancestral civilizational background. Wherever you find large contingents of such group there are always invariable problems with racism. This is an inescapable truth that progressivists reject and endeavor to cover up by blaming others for the problem. If we look at this group while inserted in the USA, an obvious assertion can be quickly made: the Black Americans that exhibit the least, if any, traits of an exacerbated sense of ethnic and racial pride are the ones that converted to Christianity. Since this religion functions under the concept of *Brotherhood in Christ*, it leads to the replacement of ethnocentrism with a worthy sense of kinship, with faith taking precedence over any superficial tribal traits such as, in this specific case, the Black race or ethnicity.

Christians look at the tribes of Israel and the first Christians, the Apostles, as being their spiritual ancestors, substituting any ancestral vacuum that is present in failed ethnic groups, such the Black African. But the peoples from this group that hang on to their vacuous past end up embracing primitive, tribalistic traits of savagery, violence, racism, incivility, etc. since this is the stage they were found at when European Christians first made contact with them in Sub-Saharan Africa. They revert into a void of ideas, principles, values, practices and very negative behavioral patterns.

White Europeans and East Asians predominantly tend to pride themselves on ancestral values, which both groups possess in abundance, allowing them to focus on intelligence, achievement, success, integrity, etc. which are a lot more significant then mere superficial traits such as ethnicity or race. Not without tensions and setbacks during integration, East Asians assimilate very easily into Western societies due to their high degree of civilizational engagement. South East-Asians don't fall much back behind.

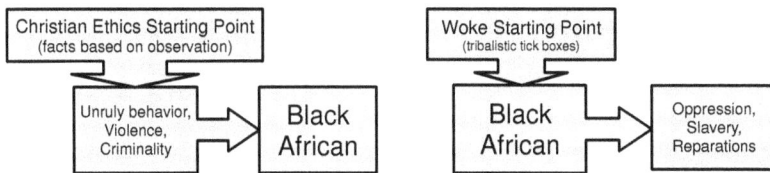

Figure 63: Ethos vs Tribalism

Looking at **Figure 63** it's far more beneficial to see race, and the other superficial human traits previously listed, as a means of identifying the problem within a group, not the cause of the problem itself. Judgment should be based on the consequences of one's behavior, not be seen as the cause that leads to their privileges or penalties. For example, if there is a high rate of crime among Black Americans, we should use the crime statistics to determine that this group has a significant issue with criminality that stands out like sore thumb, comparatively to other racial groups, as opposed to assuming their victimhood or criminality based on race. We go from facts to a low common denominator that allows us to easily identify the group, not use the group's as a low common denominator to attach a bigoted opinion based on feelings that provides convenience to an ideological narrative.

LUXURY VIRTUES

you're a prop, not a person

Atheism led to socialism as a means of leveling the economic playing field while reducing Humanity to an ant farm, which in turn led to Marxism that attempted to design a model to lead us to some sort of Heaven-on-Earth, later ending in a cultural interpretation of said ideology in the form of feminism. Eventually emotional manipulation extended itself into neo-Marxism and the postulates of *wokeness* came to be: in appreciating everything through an emotional lens societies shifted from the logical domain into pity and tear-jerking manifests. But imbued in this emotionalism another attribute typical of femalehood also rose: that of the pursuit of vanity and self-glorification through a false, superficial and self-righteous sense of virtue.

This leads us to the concept of *luxury virtues*. That would be best defined as the idea that a lot of Westerners, especially the ones that are wealthier and enjoy the vast comforts of life, have in parading the salvation of the ones they consider to be *protected groups*, such as migrants, minorities, Black Africans, the homosexual, bisexual and gender identitarians, Muslims, and any other groups they see as inferior – or under the monikers they use to hide their own bigotry, the *marginalized* and *oppressed*.

It's frequent for movie stars, pop stars and internet

influencers use, or better put, *wear* the badges of virtue and recognition once they engage in campaigns to release criminals out of jail just because of their race. Sometimes offenders that are career criminals and caused severe damage to their innocent victims are the elected for the patrons of such ritual of stupidity and ignorance – all in the name of their white savior complex. The search to employ, exult or support individuals simply based on their race, gender, sexual orientation, etc. is commonly referred to as *affirmative action*. These type of behavior garners the attention of their followers and fans, allowing the spotlight to be directly pointed at the stars, resulting in validation of a philanthropy of sorts – for self-serving purposes only obviously. The Hollywood movie industry is a clear example of where people display plentiful thirst to seek such validation through diversity hiring, more often than not resulting in very poor productions being made due to the lack of merit and value their hires possess. Oppression and victimhood tick-boxes are guaranteed not to be in shortage, however.

The importance is in utilizing the criminal or the incompetent as a means to shine, as though wearing a designer two-thousand dollar bag, shoes or any other apparel, as long as they are seen flaunting these. The amount of attention, praise and glorification are priceless. Further to this, the affluent and the ones who live a shallow, hedonistic life gain the appearance of depth, of compassion and charitable behavior. These practices can also be used to seek acquittal of previous sins, such as when an opinion had been brought forward to the public, especially by means of social media, or augment the power and protagonism of said advocate of *the cause*.

Political movements such as Black Lives Matter and their associative political parties strove on the death of criminals in the hands of the police officers in order to rake in millions by way of the latter's suffering. Effigies were built, murals were painted, leaders were elected, and all this to glorify the ones that 'fought' for the cause – nothing more than profiteers once the curtains are open revealing the truth. What used to be revered as a sign of moral nobility has been cheapened into a fashionable attribute used to convert petty, selfish, entitled, narcissistic, spoiled egocentrics into sanctimonious, illustrious icons of modern society and, as consequence, its contemporaneous ever regressive culture.

RACE AS A SOCIAL CONSTRUCT

beauty is in the mind of God

The field of forensics has evolved to the extent that today is possible to reconstruct to a certain degree of proximity the face of a person solely by using their skull, if available in its integrity. A reconstitution can be made, and it has been done so in the past, to the point of finding missing persons in cold case files. These cranial divergent characteristics were acquired by humans since the dawn of mankind and throughout it.

During the *Ice Age*, technically known as the Pleistocene Epoch, the human diaspora led us to populate every corner of the Earth. This period that encapsulates all stone age stages (Paleolithic, Mesolithic and Neolithic) lasted for over two million years, allowing for very distinct traits to be formed, shaped and chiseled for each native group of each region, in a natural process of evolution. The four groups are identified as Caucasoid, Negroid, Mongoloid and Australoid and their distribution at the end of the prehistoric period can be found in

Figure 64. These racial genetic groups themselves have been extended to split the Negroid into two (Congoid and Capoid), plus also defining Americanoid as a separate group of the Mongoloid. However they lack clear levels of distinction that the four main groups possess between each other, so they will be left out for circumspection reasons. Regardless of the merits of using six groups instead of four, the results are straightforward: it's possible to extract racial identity from a skull, defeating the idea that it's solely a social construct designed by supposedly racist White Europeans. Instead we should find this information extremely useful to better understand ourselves as a species.

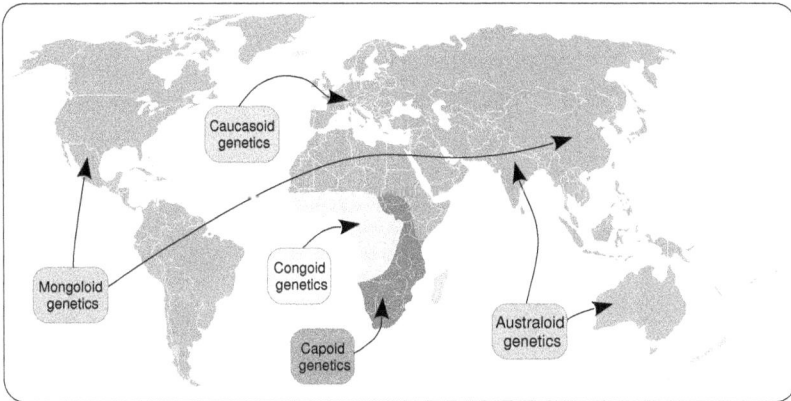

Figure 64: Racial genetic indigenous groups and their world-wide geographical distribution

Of course one cannot simply disregard the other racial genetic groups, but instead include them in the logical hierarchical structure of how race is perceived. As per **Figure 65**, *racial genetics* can be all encompassing of all races, which in turn can be broken into different sub-racial groups – better known as ethnicity – and finally these can contain divergences in skin-tonne and physiognomical traits. The latter are also know as *biological polymorphism* and denote the phenotypes based on polygenic contributions, i.e. what each human inherited from their ancestors throughout thousands of years under different environments, practices and patterns of behavior (**Figure 66**). If there are side effects, like racial tensions caused by vast improvements in our civilizational knowledge databases, we shall deal with these until we reach maturity, as opposed to running away from the truth in order to find safety in a cowardly cur, preventing a final verdict. Such is the intent of matriarchal societies where empowered women attempt to appease any grievance or disagreement by muffling the quest for intellectual and epistemological freedom.

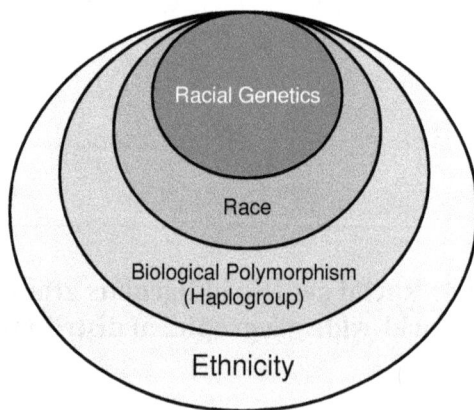

Figure 65: Racial genetics hierarchy

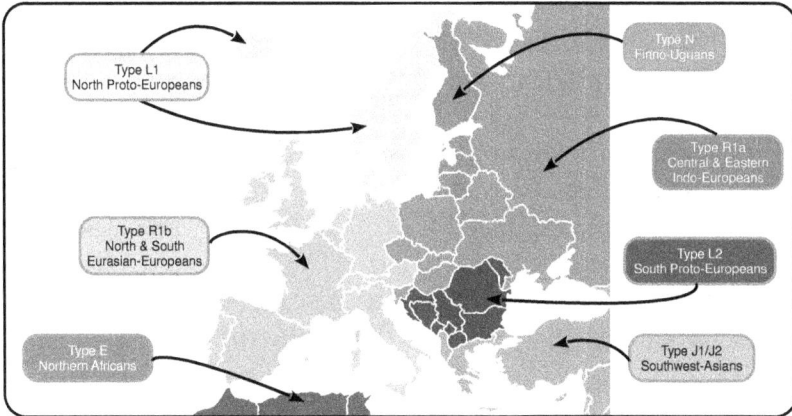

**Figure 66: Dominant Y-DNA Haplogroups (Europe, North
Africa and Southwest Asia)**

It's undeniable that humans procure to move towards divinity
as it's in our nature to abandon our primevalhood and innovate,
evolve, grow. Northern-Europeans with fair-skin, bright eyes
and fair-hair are the ones further away from our
anthropological ancestors – and also the most distant from our
cousins, the primates, in terms of appearance, and not just so.
This is an evolution ladder we want to climb in order to move
ourselves away from animality, and from what we see as
primitive and backwards. Resembling a primate is undesirable,
an insect even more so. We like to refer to ideals of beauty that
some claim to be defined by cultural environments, but in the
end of the day aren't we trying to associate ourselves with
characteristics that are mostly pleasing to us? The color blue is
that of the sky and the oceans, representing hope in our human

minds. Light skin is more agreeable in general due to the fear we have of the dark – after all we cannot see while immersed in it. This simple concepts develop in the human psyche, the collective subconscious and forever remain there substantive to our nature.

In medieval Europe, light skin was perceived as a sign of nobility, in fact the ones pertaining to the latter category were commonly designated to as *blue-blooded*, much was the veneration of people of noble birth. The justification is nobles did not work, therefore their skin was not heavily exposed to sunlight, whereas the peasantry had darker, thicker, aged skin for the very opposite reason. Today having a tan is beneficial because it reflects affluence, as the use of the beach, resorts and traveling is modernly viewed as a plus. Physical traits that are exaggerated or coarse versus soft facial features; skin that is harder to the touch versus soft baby skin; more body hair versus less hair; these and more are however less likely to relate to something sophisticated, and therefore less desirable.

These perceptions, naturally embedded in humans, can lead to discriminatory feelings or treatment – something that has happened in the past, and justifiably so since these physical and physiognomical differences were often allied with the corresponding behavioral differences and practices of its subjects. Embracing our nature and the differences imbued in it will inevitably lead to us to being a more honorable species, without neglecting what that process may involve. Persistently trying to cover up these issues by sweeping them under the rug will only increase social tensions and division. Civilizational maturity is of the utmost importance and cannot be replaced by anything else – certainly not with the fear of seeing things for what they really are, no matter what the costs or birth pains. Nevertheless this quest requires a light at the end of the tunnel, as ideals of beauty, perfection, intelligence, reason, honor, integrity, order and harmony are impossible to ignore unless we are to reject the existence an all-encompassing God.

DEMOGRAPHIC REPLACEMENT

switching off the lights

With the umbilical cord to our spiritual selves severed, atheism quickly injected *cultural relativism* into the societies it dominates. Only the ones that reached a more advanced state of derangement by attempting to redefine all social paradigms, mostly through post-modernist and post-structuralist ideas, could place themselves at the forefront of progressivist change. This occurred predominantly in the West, where neo-Marxism to this day is still metastasizing at alarming rates.

The proclivity to enter contradiction is natural to the ones that enter this realm of post-modernist subjectivity, enabling everything to be reassigned a meaning through claim or opinion. The idea that race is a social construct would inherently negate the need for *diversity:* if we are all the same why bring people from different regions of the world in first place? The lie or excuse could be protracted to disallow for cultural, culinary and religious diversity, but that is blatantly not what we witness when observing the call for open borders, globalism, mass migration and formulas to destroy the Christian Western World.

Irrespective of such fallacious argument, *diversity* keeps being pushed relentlessly into our societies under the guise of providing us with *strength*. What type of strength the neo-Marxist strategists are referring to only a truly Omniscient God would know – they certainly don't. The outcome is visible all over Europe, North America and, at a lesser scale, Australia and New Zealand: the emergence of ethnic enclaves filled with tribalism, as opposed to said *diversity*.

The new comers, sometimes of parasitical nature because they contribute in nothing towards the economy, clash with the natives of the host culture, leading to the need of the latter to often adapt to the views of the former, in a completely absurd ritual of reverse-assimilation. This pertains mostly to the large influx of immigrants from a single culture that allow for self-contained growth and little to no exposure to the hosts cultural practices and principles – were the numbers of said immigrants kept low, they would be forced to mingle with the peoples of the house they were allowed to come live in.

But what, or whom, rules the West? And how is there such voluminous under-appreciation for our Western identity and disrespect towards our forefathers and ancestral values? The deracination and degeneracy has it's roots in the aforementioned post-modernist and post-structuralist designs – to redefine one-self and restructure society, with a set of endemic and systemically oppressive identifiers is to achieve success, progress, holiness.

The desecration of our past is the dominant force of this self-flagellatory horde of cannibalistic neo-Marxists. Long gone is the Biblical Commandment to "Honor thy father and thy mother", corrupting and destroying what they can until what their own ancestors edified is nothing more than an empty, rotten carcass. Anti-White sentiment thrives, with the so called Critical Race Theory at the elm. But no matter how fancy they make it sound, how many pages of indoctrination manuals they write, it all resolves to the rudimentary Marxist formula of *oppressed vs oppressor* – this time round pitching the *people of color* – if you're not White, into the bucket you go – against the evil White esclavagist, colonialist and imperialist oppressor.

Complete dismissal of the fact that White European Christians were the ones that ended slavery and, due controlling three-quarters of the globe when doing so, enforced such concept worldwide is the only way to explain the clear display of anachronistic arrogance: nothing more than the act of current generations attacking their ancestors using values and principles that were provided to the them by those very ancestors. These standards are being incorrectly taken for granted as self-evident – a bit like traveling back in time ten thousand years to mock people for not utilizing the wheel before it was invented, even if it's the people that lived around that period were the ones that came up with the idea. Had these SJW, Woke or neo-Marxists been born two-hundred years ago for example, they would have no idea that slavery is bad and would likely own slaves themselves, if given the chance. The sheer nerve to use the precepts their own ancestors ascertained and fought for, only to mark them as evil. Slavery was ubiquitous and ever-present in the history of humans, before Europeans changed the rules of the game during the colonization era. Not to mention the fact that the vast majority of slaves were sold by African slavers who had been operating for over a thousand years in the Arab slave trade – are reparations to be asked from Arabs and the Muslim? What about the the African slaver's descendants, should they pay too? After all most of the slaves that were brought into the New World were purchased, not captured as can be seen on **Figure 67**, therefore requiring some sharing of the blame.

The self-loathing that Westerners, especially the younger generations and predominantly female, have been brain-washed and indoctrinated to hold in them is an attempt to dismantle the Christian West and succeed it with a globalist empire. It relates in no way to virtue, justice, *diversity* or *equity*. If the Christian Global Empire that withstood five-hundred years collapses, many of today's concepts and ideas that are taken for granted, such as sovereignty of the state, sovereignty of the individual, Human Rights, nation state borders, free-market economies, private ownership, cultural identity and much more, will collapse with it. A global totalitarian conglomerate will certainly have no interest in preserving any of these.

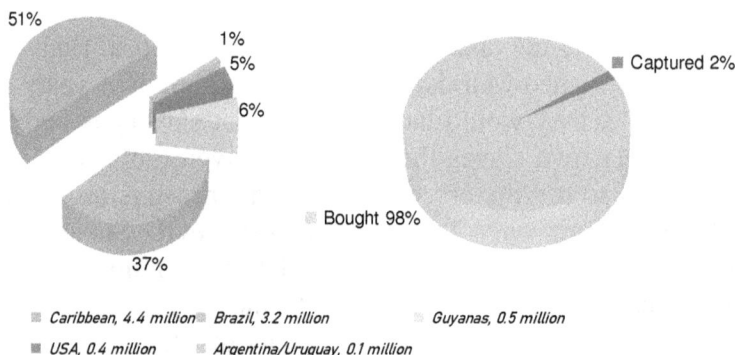

51%
1%
5%
6%
37%

Captured 2%
Bought 98%

Caribbean, 4.4 million   Brazil, 3.2 million   Guyanas, 0.5 million
USA, 0.4 million   Argentina/Uruguay, 0.1 million

Figure 67: Trans-Atlantic African slave trade

The unmistakable truth is that the human species has always been diverse. We don't need this artificially injected *diversity*, as it does not constitute strength, as *real* strength comes from freedom, knowledge, social cohesion, ancestral pride, individual worth and other traits that were predominant up until atheism started replacing Christianity and its values and principles across modern Western societies.

GLOBALISM

open casket

Immigration should always be based on the scrutinous process of evaluating each candidate's to integrate and contribute to the host society they wish to migrate into. Disregard for such concept will lead to societal and cultural harm, due to the entry of undesired individuals coming from cultures where failure and misbehavior is rampant, hence the need for the migratory process. One could say that if all countries were successful due to adopting ideas and practices that align with a successful ethos as well as scientific and technological achievement and therefore flourished, there would be no need for immigration other than for the reshuffling of people based on their individual skill sets.

You could have a country with a shortage of medical doctors, who in turn would have a surplus of engineers where the migratory process would make sense without any need for pity or baby-sitting involved. Migration would then be the result of exchange, import and export of skills in order to balance the productivity of each society. Another factor could be an individual's preference of particular characteristics of a culture versus the one they grew up in – but again, the migratory arrangement would have to deem them to be an added asset to the host culture that would accept him, as opposed to some sort of systemic sympathy parade as we can find occurring in the current Western countries, an advent of the modern Woke culture.

The concept of successful countries having to carry the weight of the world in their shoulders is purely a feminine concept, brought forward by the current sickness of the West, and the plague that is leading us back to the cave – feminism. There is no rational explanation one could give to justify such intent under a logical lens. Indeed it must be asked, why should cultures, ethnic groups and the people's of booming civilizations have to bring over hordes of uncivilized groups from unsuccessful ones?

There is but one reason, and an emotional one: pity. The female Homo-sapiens task was always primarily that of care-giving, of tending to the weak, that is themselves and, most of all, their children. When put in a position of power women will inevitably revert to their own motherly instinct which is so dominant in their being. It's self-defeating to consider otherwise. This would explain why there is always a focus on naming illegal immigrants as *refugees*, which a term that has lost all its meaning. Originally the sentiment was that of aiding people in a strict, meticulous process that may be in need of aid offered by a free-spirited Christian society, where rules are based on principles such as those of personal freedoms and equality. An individual clearly identified as someone persecuted for reasons that would be condemnable by the Christian ethos could then be provided shelter and protection under Western rule. But instead the system was emphatically abused by the *feel goodists* (feminists, wokes and alike), which utilized it to pour into the thriving West large numbers of people who cause disruption. It appears to be a means of punishment for daring to be so healthy and successful where otherwise there is so much misery and poverty in the world – the typical socialist epitaph of achieving equality by making everyone equally miserable. The latter loves company after all.

This is a mindset very much entirely based on the female brain with the pursuit of dysgenics as a form of evening the system. A very simple analogy of such mindset would be that of a chicken-mother ensuring and its chicks have the same number of grains by taking the *excess* from the one that was abundantly served and redistributing it evenly across all the others. Makes sense at this level due to the limited context we find ourselves in, where there is an emotional bond, a spiritual proximity. However this proves disastrous when such conditions aren't met and is paramount of female behavior leading to the Matriarchal Shift as mentioned in a previous chapter. In the large World context such mentality proves irredeemably calamitous. Men built and led civilization under a completely different mental framework, that of *reason* where one's ability to interact with reality in the most efficient manner took precedence over *emotion,* which came in a distant second.

On could put this to the test and present the hypothesis of Western countries bringing over millions of African migrants out of pity: 100 million go into Europe, the same amount into North America, and one-fifth of that into Oceania (Australia/New Zealand). Africa currently has over 1.4 billion people, so subtract the 220 million and you would have well over a billion. Add in the estimate that Africa should cross over 2.5 billion people, using current growth rates statistics, by the turn of the 22nd century. The results are clear: not only would we overpopulate the West with people that would cause extreme disruption, if not total annihilation of what used to be the flourishing Christian Liberal Economies, but what change would that bring to Africa? Instead of reaching the estimate 2.5 billion population within the next 80 years maybe they would settle for 2.3 billion. How is that any different? Would there be no wars, gangsterism, barbarity and animality that currently pervades the African continent? Wouldn't there be plenty of new children starving to death all the same? Wouldn't there be still child labor and prostitution. What would have been fixed or resolved? Absolutely nothing. And at the same time the Christian West would also collapse due to the excess of population alone, not to mention the importation of all the problems that such demographics would comprise of.

In the early 1970s the Indian population was set at around 500 million. Fast-forward to today and it has rose to an astounding 1.5 billion. This latter number is without taking into account the over 30 million Indians that are estimated to have migrated out of India in the last five or six decades. Shall we engage in the same exercise as we did with Africa? Now one must clarify that the backwardness of India and its culture is in no way comparable to that of African ones, especially Sub-Saharan, but that does not leave much space to contest the obvious reality: there is a blatant disregard for humanity, and their own Indian peoples, in allowing such massive, chaotic birth-rates. Not only it will soon be incomportable for the planet to have so many inhabitants within just a few decades but this is also blatant disrespect and disdain for any civilized cultures that don't engage in such endemic behavior.

Regardless, let's engage in the same exercise as before and bring over one billion people out of India into the West. Certainly the latter would collapse instantly into a pit of third-world overpopulation, scarcity of resources, corruption, social inequalities and inequities, only to find out that in another mere 50 years India would have fully replenished its population by one extra billion. If this has happened before in such a restricted timeline (from the early 1970s until the present day), certainly there would be no impediment for it to happen all over again, even if it were to take a little longer.

One could say there is no such attempt at bringing this voluminous numbers into the Western societies, but then the question arises: what are the low numbers for? What is their value and what do they signify? Will they solve poverty in Africa? Overpopulation in the Indian subcontinent? Corruption in Central America? No, none of these but they will certainly make our Western females and the Woke cultists *feel good*. No rime, no reason, no rational or logical process – just feelings, through a momentary injection of dopamine certainly and, even worse, the flavor of self-gratification and self-edification, or as it is currently known, *virtue signaling*. The spotlight is pointed at them: "Look at me!", they shout, drawing attention to all the flags and banners they carry, all the pronouns they announce and all the people they are *altruistically* trying to save! The cause for such display is entirely a manifestation of sanctimonious, self-serving egoism and self-absorption, as that of overgrown babies seeking validity in a world of grown-ups. A world built by adults that strive through hard-work and productivity, not acephalous childish games and play-making. Were these immature imbeciles fruitful, hard-working members of society engaging in effort and breaking sweat, certainly such self-indulgent and immature behavior wouldn't ensue, therefore avoiding the demise of the most successful civilization that Humanity has ever seen.